ON FIRE

The battle of Genoa and
the anti-capitalist movement

**ONE-OFF
PRESS**

This book is dedicated to all those struggling against capitalism

ISBN 1 902593 54 5

Published by One Off Press
Distributed through AK Distribution and Active Distribution
September 2001

C O N T E N T S

INTRODUCTION

This is a book about militant protest—to be more precise, the militant response of sections of the anti-G8 demonstrations in Genoa in July 2001. This book aims to give you an insight into the ideas and actions behind the confrontational approach of these militants. This approach has been described as a violent approach—we think violence is too strong a word, it's a word that should be reserved for our enemies. Our violence is a drop in the ocean when compared to their violence. We prefer to call it a confrontational approach. A confrontational approach means that we are prepared to confront the violence of the police and the violence of the system.

The world leaders of that system present a glowing example to the rest of the planet. Of the eight men who met in Genoa in July, one seized the presidency of his country after losing the election. Another is pursuing a genocidal war in an annexed republic. A third is facing allegations of corruption. A fourth, the summit's host, has been convicted of illegal party financing, bribery and false accounting, while his right hand man is on trial for consorting with the Mafia. Hardly any of them have an electoral mandate of more than a quarter of their populations. But despite this reality, the major theme of the Genoa G8 summit was "promoting democracy". However, those in the streets outside had different ideas...

The articles in this book have either been taken from reports posted on the internet or from contacting individuals who were present in Genoa. Due to the need to have this book out as soon as possible, reports have primarily come from either UK or American sources. We are sure that people from other countries—especially, of course, Italy—would have both similar and different experiences. There is not a particular 'party' line and we include articles that contain differing points of view. The aim of this book is to encourage debate about theory and tactics so as to empower us to take on those who currently are ruling this world. We are not victims, we are not sheep, we all have the ability to be active participants in our own destinies. We hope that the contents will inspire you.

One Off Press
September 2001

> > G L O S S A R Y

ANARCHISTS People who believe the word would be better off without constituted authority. An odd bunch of critters ranging from the intelligent and thoughtful to raving weirdoes.

BLACK BLOCK A protest tactic in which a section of a demo is formed by whoever turns up wearing black clothes and usually masks. Invented by European anarchists to counter police surveillance.

CAPITALISM A peculiar, but inexplicably successful (for a tiny group of people) economic theory whose proponents purport to believe that when an economic system ensures that those who already rich get richer without working, everyone is better off. Usually associated with drugs, limited intelligence and firearms.

CARABINIERI A formal Italian police faction under military command equivalent to the French Gendarmes or the British Territorial Support Group. Armed and nasty. Other Italian police forces include the state police, municipal police, financial police and penitentiary police.

G8 A body representing the world's leading nation-states (Canada, France, Germany, Japan, Italy, Russia, United Kingdom and United States of America). Also includes both formally and informally representatives from corporations and other organisations.

GENOA A port in northern Italy which liberated itself from the Nazis in the second world war. Later it was chosen to be the site for the annual G8 summit.

GSF Genoa Social Forum—the umbrella group who coordinated the G8 protests. Primarily liberal (see below) in approach.

GLOBALISATION A trendy euphemism for neo-colonialism. The imposition of the agenda of western business leaders on everyone else by force, bribery or other forms of skulduggery.

LIBERALS Sometimes well meaning, sometimes deluded people who believe that capitalism can be made slightly nicer by asking for a few more crumbs. They fail to understand the fundamental nature of capitalist society.

RED ZONE Area where the G8 were meeting in Genoa, surrounded by 20,000 heavily armed police officers and a 5m high fence.

SOCIALIST WORKERS PARTY Small political group who reject neo-colonialism in favour of the imposition of the agenda of western Marxist leaders on everyone else by selling newspapers and other forms of skulduggery.

PINK BLOCK A section of a demo composed of people using costumes and theatre to create a carnival atmosphere.

TUTE BIANCHE Translates as 'white overalls'. A direct action group born out of campaigns against the casualisation of labour. Wear white and indulge in physical, but largely symbolic attacks on the police.

YA BASTA Anti neo-liberal international solidarity group inspired by the Zapatista rebellion in Mexico. Members often also involved in Tute Bianche.

> > O N E

shooting blanks?

by D I E G O J O N E S

'The danger of the 'moderate' view, which refuses to contemplate the sheer
rapacity of western state power, is that it can be co-opted. The World Bank
and the IMF, now under siege as never before, have devised their survival
tactics in relation to this' ***John Pilger***

I went to Genoa—hoping there would be a revolution, I knew there wasn't really a possibility of that but at least we might be able to force the leaders from the eight most powerful countries to flee for their lives, that would be a big step in the right direction.

My life has been a struggle, growing up and living in a Northern English city, trying to get by day to day, watching my mother being ground into an early grave, when I was a teenager, by hard work, and watching the marks of hardship and pain on my father's face; in his 70s now, he still works to supplement his meagre pension. I've watched the rest of my family work and struggle year in year out. I remember us all as kids, laughing and playing makeshift bingo, for chocolates my ma had brought home from work. I look at them now, and they look old and worn out. Their lives make me think of a hamster on a wheel, always running but never going anywhere, slowing down as they get older and more tired, knowing that if they stop and then fall off, their whole lives will collapse around them. Life—for most of us—means no matter how hard we work, we are always just one step away from losing it all. Being political from an early age can be hard, because you understand more why you are struggling and that others are benefiting from it. You also learn not to turn on the person next to you and blame them for your troubles, for your poverty. You have

compassion and empathy for the people you see trying to get by, to pay their bills, to keep the gas and electricity men and the bailiffs from the door. But at the same time you know who the enemy is but you can't see them, the people responsible for this struggling. It is difficult to not feel hatred and bitterness when you begin to put the many questions that keep you awake at night together, and realise that you, your families, your friends and the people around you, all these lives are geared towards serving the interests of someone else.

As the years went on I become more and more aware of how both the local and the global economy works. I studied in great detail the history of the slave trade, the destruction of native life in the Americas, British imperialism and colonialism— US post war foreign policy. I observed for years, the activities of death squads funded by the US, I read about poor people in the Third World being murdered for trying to make a decent life for themselves, a life free from the rich parasites in their own country and the US parasites above them. In the UK in the eighties I was involved in resisting the full frontal attack by the Thatcher government and the police on working class communities. I saw life becoming harder and harder for people I cared for. I saw the political spirit and the inner spirit of people I grew up with flitter away. Drugs flooded the area, and the only answer became instead of fighting back—to turn to escape, or turn on each other. I saw communities turn in on themselves. I have been trying to reach into people and give them that spirit back. I have been trying to convince them that by getting together and fighting back that life could be different. That this drastic move from some semblance of a community spirit into a soulless, cultureless world can be stopped and that there are people responsible for these changes, responsible for the reduction and quality of our lives.

This new movement that has been developing since Seattle has lifted that spirit a little, it still needs to go a long way, and every community, in every town and city in the world needs to be reached. Our job at least in this city is to reach out to as many people as possible—here—to try and challenge the corporate views and the corporate media. I came to Genoa to be with people, who like me, felt that intense rage against inequality and injustice and also because there were other people there who were my enemies, who were meeting there to discuss how best to serve their interests better and to continue to screw the rest of us over. I wanted to feel that solidarity that warmth of people like me and I also wanted some outlet for my anger, and they as the most powerful politicians in the world seemed a justifiable target.

My first port of call was the Carlini Stadium, the place where those who were carrying out civil-disobedience were staying. The atmosphere was great. I, and the people I was with, got to know people from all over the world there, in the few days before the demos, we eat together, laughed together and all shared the same sleeping space. The place was largely occupied by Ya Basta. I had met some people from Ya Basta before when I visited the Leoncavallo Social Centre in Milan, I was extremely impressed—and they came across to me as a well-organised group who were part and parcel of the local community. On one of the social events there, a Saturday night, the main hall, cafes and outdoor bars were full, there was around 10,000 people there, most of them I would say were local people—this was no ghetto. Even watching them have their meetings in the centre, you could see many people there were just ordinary local people, people of all ages. I couldn't understand what was being discussed though. I had also heard about Ya Basta in Prague—they worked like a huge affinity group, at a level I had never witnessed; they seemed more organised in confrontational situations than anyone else.

This time though the problem was despite having contact with them over a period of months prior to Genoa, I was beginning to discover that there was very little room for outsiders. Also they were having meetings to which no-one else was invited—so if you wanted to participate in the civil disobedience march, then you did it on their terms. Which I suppose has a certain amount of logic in it—and they had been practising for months for this assault on the Red Zone. But I also felt that very little information was being shared out, so there was no room for debate—and for an old timer like me, with lots of experience of organising and police confrontation this was difficult to swallow. Their structure did seem to be very authoritarian, but let's not label them as just another lefty group; the people I have met from Ya Basta are good people, they are not your twee middle class arrogant Trots or Leninists. They are well known and respected amongst ordinary people at least in Milan and Rome where I visited them. They are prepared to take action, and not make excuse after excuse and backtrack again and again like the SWP and all the other British 'vanguard' parties—there is no comparison. Ya Basta I have respect for. They show you solidarity and they have a wealth of experienced activists, many people dating back to the Red Brigades, some even further. We have a lot to learn from Ya Basta— especially how they organise their protests, and they also have a large percentage of women in their organisation, very confident women, which is good to see. But they are authoritarian, and it was difficult to not believe that when I visited them earlier on in the year, they had only shown me what they wanted to show me—and it was also difficult to get any answers or anything done in Carlini, unless you spoke to their leaders, Luca or Eva.

Realising along with many other people in Carlini that our only role on the Ya Basta section of the march would be at the rear, being ordered about—we decided we would have to do something else. The problem I had with this was that no one else had organised anything—the Anarchist groups had not set anything up. Which pissed me off. I knew that if a few thousand like-minded people were coming to my city, I would have done everything to welcome them or to make action plans. Maybe the Italian Anarchists were worried, that when the teargas had died down, the police would come looking for them and we would all be gone. I was also despondent at first, at the prospect of anarchists from outside of Italy, trying to organise actions without the guidance of the Genoa Anarchists, especially since the Anarchists there had not set up any sort of structure, no legal nor first aid support. And I wasn't to impressed with the 'International Anarchist offensive', at that point: apart from the Greeks and maybe a handful of others, the rest I came across were just the fashion anarchists, either punks or swampies. So initially I had decided to go on the Pink section, fearing the Black Block would end in total disaster, with people just taking desperate measures, getting nicked then looking at 10-year sentences. The Pink section in itself was Anarchist but in a sort of comedy confrontational way. It wasn't until the first civil disobedience march started and I released I hadn't come all this way to simply sing songs, have a laugh and take the piss out of the cops—I wanted something serious to happen, something that would scare the shit out of the G8 leaders. These bastards were fucking over our lives good and proper, they didn't give a toss about the fact that life was getting harder and harder for people, they just wanted their bank balances to get bigger and for their power to increase. And there they were, less than a mile away, content in their smugness—knowing full well that 18,000 cops and military were kissing their arses, preparing to do their dirty work. It was then, when around 2,000 of the so-called black block arrived, (I say 'so-called' because many of them were not in black) complete with a marching band that my true allegiance and anger came to the surface. I, along with a number of people I was with, left the Pink Section. I pulled my hat, scarf, gas mask and black T-shirt out my pockets (I had big pockets) and in amongst the crowd changed my appearance.

Within about 30 seconds, I heard a loud bang, I was pretty shocked at first—it was only about 12 noon, and the other sections of the demo weren't starting until after 1pm. I turned and saw about ten people hitting the windows of a bank, with anything they could get their hands on, with the bank alarm soon echoing around the street. One guy had picked up an iron bar from somewhere and was whacking it into the glass; another guy without a mask or anything ran up to the shutters (don't know why only two had been pulled down) and started violently punching them. I approached, when he stepped back and offered him the spare scarf I had (ever seen Fagin from *Oliver* with the pockets that go on and on?). After a few minutes the windows began to crack. I looked around for something else to attack—some symbol of wealth, but along the street—I recognised nothing that could be identified as a symbol of wealth—only little shops, chemists, photography shops, tobacconists. Within a few minutes all the windows of the bank were broken but the guys carried on hitting them; I couldn't understand why, I thought the plan was to break the windows. But soon I realised—they wanted to get into the bank!! A couple of guys got through the window, then re-appeared with computers and files throwing them onto the street, this I hoped would mess up the bank for at least for a few weeks, and maybe create more employment in the process—shame there was no money to throw out onto the street. The whole scene was pretty chaotic, part of the crowd was going down one street looking for legitimate targets, I think, the other part down another street, and the riot cops approaching us from the direction of the Red Zone, while the police helicopter appeared, hovering over the top of us. Some people began to turn recycling bins over, so they could get at the bottles, other people began to run down the road towards the police chucking them; within seconds teargas was hitting the floor in front of the crowd; people began to run in all different directions, as I was walking backward down a street watching the police, one lad threw a brick through a car at the side of the road, which really pissed me off, I approached him, but he disappeared in the crowd. I along with others managed to stop another guy from trying to smash up a bus shelter. This was different than the plans I had—that type of mindless vandalism that affects ordinary people really pisses me off. Most people didn't know where to go next, teargas was everywhere. Luckily I'd brought a few lemons, to rub on my stinging face, but my eyes were all bleared, and I'd lost my bottle of water. No-one looked like they really knew what to do. I'd also realised I'd lost sight of the people I was with, in the chaos; all around me were languages I couldn't understand. In Britain on situations like this, you see a lot of people you know, and you feel much safer, because you know people are looking out for you. Amongst the people here I didn't know anyone. I'd been to Nice and had noticed a lot of ETA and PKK people on the 'black block' section, that was weird—just cos they are prepared to take the fight a few steps further, particularly against the cops—and I don't know what their philosophy is about attacking solely legitimate targets. And they are prepared to die for their cause—I'm not sure if I was. I tried to find the people I knew in the crowd. Meanwhile the cops were approaching up the road, and they were volleying gas canisters everywhere. No-one seemed to know what to do or where to go. We used to have a policy when attacking fascist gatherings in other cities that we would allow those who knew the area to guide us, and collective decisions would be made easier, by one of our group volunteering (someone we trusted), to be a link to decision-making. They would make a decision they felt we would agree with—then report back to us and we would follow that decision. In urgent situations it works much better than always having big meetings, which are not always possible. Here possibly because of lack of local activists, nobody seemed to have a plan—not a plan of escape, not a plan of attack. I followed people going down dead ends—or small roads that could be easy prey for the cops, especially with the helicopter hovering overhead. Not being able to find anyone I knew, I figured this was gonna end in a bad way. I decided to count my losses and disappear. I walked off around a corner, whipped my mask, scarf and T-shirt off and walked away from the chaos. I thought of trying to find the Pink group again. I was frustrated—I didn't want to just voice my opposition, I wanted to send a shiver right through their black souls just like we done with Thatcher at the poll tax uprising, the way we done with the fascists at Waterloo. It was only later that I realised it hadn't gone as bad as I'd imagined, and that people had not been defeated easily by the cops. Maybe I should have trusted the old saying 'out of chaos comes order' and that people can be more effective when no-one is leading them, and they can act better both individually and in a group. That day a lot of brave people threw themselves into dangerous and confrontational situations, not because they were full of hate, as the media would have us believe, but because like me they were against hate and wanted a better world. Carlo was one of them; he was killed on his feet, fighting the machinery of obedience, hate and oppression.

I wandered through the streets which were surprisingly deserted, trying to find the rest of the demo. I began to respect what someone had told me earlier—how important it is to acclimatise yourself to a city. I didn't know where the fuck I was—I didn't know how to get to a train station, how to get out of the city, how to get away from the cops—should I need to. I tried to work out some route; every now and again I would stop and look back, and even with each street I walked down, I got further and further away yet I would still see clouds of smoke rising above the buildings. While I was lost I ended up at the fences and a gate into the Red Zone, in a street that was completely deserted. Only two cops were standing guard. I sat down in a square, trying to gain my bearings. I saw three guys parking up a car, in front of the fence and looking really terrified, they shifted a couple of boxes of stuff out of the boot and placed them by the cops inside the Red Zone, then one guy got back in the car and drove off really quick, while the others disappeared with the boxes in the Red Zone. It was funny to see; there was no one around yet these guys were shitting themselves. I saw another guy walk out of the Red Zone and immediately remove a label off his jacket, he too looked incredibly nervous—it was good to see. If these guys were terrified, imagine how the G8 leaders felt, knowing that people would recognise them. So when Blair, Bush or Berlusconi or any of the other gangsters come on the TV, and pretend that these anti-capitalists are not bothering them, don't believe them—the bastards are shitting themselves, that's why they killed Carlo to scare us off.

Eventually after about an hour, I arrived at a road that was overlooking the railway tracks and across the other side was the road leading from Carlini to Brignole Station, by the Red Zone. This was where I figured Ya Basta would be marching down, in their thousands, dressed in their padded gear and riot helmets and heading straight for the Red Zone (I'd decided to first check whether my mates had left the 'black block' and had gone back to the Pink Group; if I knew they were OK I would then join Ya Basta as they came down the road). I then bumped into a Greek guy I knew from Carlini Stadium, who like me had been separated from his friends, and left the 'black block'. Within about 15 minutes we had found the Pink group, or what was left of it. Everything was chaotic—the Pink group seem to have ended up with the Peace group, the demo for them seemed to be over, people were just sitting around, chatting. I'd heard they had been water cannoned and tear gassed too. But I couldn't find any of my friends. I arrived in a square where people were making webs out of some weird sticky material—I wondered what the point of it was. I walked up one

street then down another. Suddenly at the top of one of the roads, I saw some commotion, I saw tear gas, and people with scarves, dressed in black running towards me, most of them were women, a couple of them tried to make a makeshift barricade with bins. Some of the peace people started forming a line across the road, and as the people in black reached them, they blocked their way, telling them they couldn't come down this way. I got really angry with them and started arguing, but none of them claimed to speak English. The people in black ran off in another direction, I walked quickly up to the top of the road, to see what was going on. When I reached there, the smell of tear gas was in the air, but people just seemed to be sitting around on the grass, there were stalls and some people playing music—I saw a load of 'Globalise Resistance' people just sitting around looking like a bunch of boy scouts or brownies on an outing, with stupid looking red cravats around their necks. I then saw a group of people who I knew from the Pink group, walking through the street; they said they were going to join Ya Basta who were going down to Brignole station. I followed them. In the near distance, below me, across the railway lines the air was thick with CS gas and I could see what looked like thousands of people charging the police—I couldn't believe it had all happened so quick, I tried to summon the people who were sitting around, but no-one seemed interested. We must have walked down around 100 steps—when we arrived on the street, a street I had passed about an hour previously, this time it looked like a war had just ended. People were standing around on street corners looking bemused, there were cars, petrol stations, shops burnt out, with their windows smashed, I saw people sitting around drinking beers and eating food, then I passed a supermarket that had been smashed and was still being looted. I saw what looked like local people coming out holding shopping bags full of goods. There were empty gas shells all over the road. But not a cop in sight. Many people were just going about their daily routine, as if nothing had happened; it was bizarre—I wondered whether I'd been drifting through the streets of Genoa on some astral plane (not really) but I don't know how I'd missed it. Around the corner I could see the battle from below, with Ya Basta trying to push forward trying to get to the Red Zone. I crossed the bridge over the railway line.

The streets were full of empty CS gas canisters, bits of sticks, paper and torn makeshift armoury and people, about 15,000 of them, charging the cops, many of them in crash helmets, and homemade body armour. I was somewhere in the middle but in front of me I could see people going for it at the front. I noticed that neither a shop nor a bus shelter had been touched. I knew the street didn't have symbols of wealth, I'd been passing it everyday on my way to the convergence centre—this was a poor area, and people, 15,000 of them, had respected that. This was important to me; life was hard enough for most of us. I got back into T-shirt and gas mask, and moved forward. I had nothing for my eyes though, they were stinging like fuck, plus the heat was intense. I kept a look out for the people I'd come down with. We moved forward, and despite the CS gas we still moved forward. I saw Ya Basta, holding up these huge shields to block the persistent CS gas coming over the top from the police lines and gas canisters being chucked onto the railway line (there were people with gloves picking them up and either chucking them back at the cops or over onto the railway line). My Greek friend reappeared next to me, (I wondered how he recognised me) and said he'd seen someone get hit in the head with a gas canister, and he saw them collapse with blood squirting from their head. We still pushed forward, I suddenly found myself not far from the front, and I could see—despite the huge machinery and armoury of the police, people were brave enough to fight them. Suddenly people started backing off, I stood there, I could hardly see but was trying to find something to chuck at the cops. Even worse, people started running, I stopped in the crowds to see what was going on, but everyone was running past me, knocking into me, away from the police—I suddenly saw what looked like something out of star wars, a huge grey tank thing, driving straight at the crowds, and right behind this huge thing were cops in the armoured vehicles. I started running. Fuck, I thought—to my left was the railway line, with a huge drop, everybody seemed to be running faster than me, I think I must have been near the back, I needed to run quicker, I'd break my legs if I tried to jump over onto the railway line, I ran like hell, but the bastards were catching up. Suddenly I saw to my left a grass verge that was leading up from the side of the railway lines. I had to reach there—otherwise I've had it, ten years and I haven't even done anything yet. The cops are fuckin mad, I don't know how they didn't kill anyone, and I don't know how I got up on the wall. I was about to jump, when I saw an old fella trying to run, I shouted to him to get on the wall, I jumped down, and helped him up, and as I got back on the wall, the water-cannon hit the both of us, we went tumbling down into the trees and nettles, I had to just grab at anything, some sharp prickly branches, to stop myself from falling further. Then a gas canister was fired almost on top of us. We got up really quick, I thought the cops would follow over the wall after us, and I slid down what looked like an embankment. I looked around and saw that quite a few people had taken the same route. I was soaked to the bone with just that one blast. Luckily for us the cops didn't follow us, they carried on up the road after the mass of protesters. I waited for about a minute with the others. Everyone was coughing, and trying to blow their nose, my bastard eyes were killing me. There were a few Italian women with us, who went round everyone, spraying them with this special stuff that eases the sting on the skin. When things had calmed down, and my eyes cleared up, I took a peek over the wall, and saw a few vanloads of riot cops to the left of me, across the road, and they had about 10 demonstrators lined up against the wall, they were looking over towards us. Some people took a path down by the railway lines, I took my black T-shirt off, shoved everything in my pockets, waited for about five minutes, then stepped back on the road, I looked up the road but could see nothing. I heard later that the police were trying to force Ya Basta back to Carlini, I couldn't see what part I could play now—so I wandered off (I was fairly confident—the cops wouldn't think I was a demonstrator, I look too normal).

The rest of our group had agreed to meet, if we got split up, at the convergence centre so I headed down there. But I got a bit lost and came in along the east side of the bay, the side where the wealthy lived and played. It was this area that would be destroyed the next day. Their boutiques and restaurants would be burned out. Later I heard of Carlo's death. And seeing his body the next day on the front page of the newspapers, it didn't make me sick, just sad and angry. I thought this is it—the battle is on, I know Carlo won't be the last one. I thought of how we would get revenge, maybe attack the cop shop.

The next day on the march of 300,000—I tried to find action, tried to start action. The closest we got was jumping up and down on a huge ship container taunting the police and when a group of about 50 of us walked past hundreds of cops, guarding the main police headquarters and copshop, all we could do was stare at them. I must have set off at the wrong time or something, because I didn't know or see any of the banks getting burnt, until I passed them later on my way up to the media centre. I missed that, I even missed the attack on the Diaz school by about 30 minutes, I was glad of that though. I felt something strange in the air. When I got back to England I felt frustrated, I wished I'd got stuck in more—I'd have something else to tell my kids, something they would be proud of, that's when I have kids. One thing though, despite the fact that some groups organised for months for the demo, and the black block only got it together a couple of days before, their actions were the ones that caused more damage and sent more fear through the hearts of the G8 and the cops, and hit the headlines, making people think again about the term anti-capitalist. One thing though—that's no excuse for not getting better-organised next time.

> > T W O

reporting from the frontline

by BRIAN S

July 20th update... Genoa... what the hell is going on (this is a personal report, and while some of the info in here is based on rumours, it is true to the best of my knowledge and should at least give you an idea of what's happening here).

Would like to say that it is absolute insanity here... but really it's getting to be quite common. The anti-capitalist fight has certainly stepped up a notch (concerning western activist summit-hopping).

Streets are filled with debris and fire. Roving bands of riot cops from the centre clash with thousands of activists back and forth all over the city. There is confirmation now that one person has died in the fights (by being hit by police vans charging crowds at high speed) and another is waiting to be confirmed. Tear gas is everywhere, over a hundred thousand people are taking to the streets all over the city.

When one gathering of several thousand is scattered or one decides to leave, you can find 10,000 more just a few streets over, gaining space on the police. No-one has made it through the Red Zone, but that doesn't quite matter. It's a war against the state and its soldiers down here. (As I write this I hear someone beside me confirming photos of a person being shot by the military police... reports of 72 wounded).

Quick look at what the day looked like for me... After the late night of rain and campsite floodings, people woke up early in there various places. Generally groups gathered in the east and headed west to try to break through the Red Zone, some going south, and others heading straight on or to the north.

Early reports came of the socialist blocks under heavy watercannon fire somewhere within the tightened south zone. By noon, large shipping containers (for boats and trains) had been moved to completely block off many streets in the yellow area. Pink block consisting of determined samba bands and fiesta moved north to join the women's action and other NGOs.

Atmosphere there was largely festive of course and reports have come through the day of sit-ins with large arrests and teaming up with the sections of the black block to clash with the cops. Tute Bianche and other civil disobedience types marched from their far off staging area straight down the main road towards Brignole station.

One section of black block left from our camp who we travelled with. Perhaps 3,000. We marched east and met with the militant trade union COBAS and other anarcho syndicalist groups. At the union downtown bank windows began to be smashed... it was not long before we could see tear gas up ahead and other groups clashing with police.

From here on it was back and forth for me and many others. Advance a block, mix with protestors from another groups, have police beat us back, and then head back or by another route. Around noonish when we first arrived we were finally pushed back up the eastern hill near Piazza Tomamase and eventually scattered down side streets.

Making our way towards the indymedia we found dumped garbage bins everywhere and even a turned car, this area was soon to be controlled by lots of cops. Next we headed down to the convergence point at the water. As we got there, police were starting to move in.

The main entrances had been barricaded by remnants of COBAS and the Black Block to keep the police from invading. We got in a side way. As we entered, the majority of demonstrators were leaving and heading along the water. We stayed on to get some food with other random people and were invaded by police again.

Military style riot cops began single filing over the barricades to get in. After they had entered, and the hundred of food workers in side were barricading their restaurants, a police tank/bulldozer came through and tore down the barricades. The police then did some fancy manoeuvres and realising there weren't many folks there, took off again.

After an hour or so we walked up through Piazza Rosetti and north to see if we could find the Tute Bianche. It was a strange feeling. People wandering around, some sitting in front of rows of riot cops with banners. Others lounging on grass, and just random walkers. We headed through the district and past many police lines which just watched us with little interest and tried to be intimidating.

It seems sometimes safest to walk in small groups here. Eventually we ran into several thousand anarchists having a pitched street battle with the cops. We stayed around for a while. More dumpsters on fire, the streets filled with broken glass. During this battle, a police van went nuts and started charging in to break past the dumpster barricades.

At first people ran but then the van was surrounded and was being beaten back by rocks and other projectiles. The armoured van tried several times but was eventually beaten far back with thousands of protestors chasing it and yelling victory cheers. Just then another police line down a side street disintegrated and was beaten

away by protestors advancing from another direction.

I left this battle shortly and went to see what was happening a few streets over. I walked out and saw maybe another 10,000 people down Via Tolemaic who had completely taken over. All of them were padded with makeshift armour and taking turns pushing forward.

One really amazing thing that was happening in these battles was that every time the police charged with tear gas, many people would start running. But those behind, instead of joining, would put their hand in the air and remind in a gentle way... "tranquillo, calma, stay calm". And it worked, people would slow down, realise it was just tear gas and then return to the fray...

Well... this is getting long... but basically it was going on like this for several hours back and forth. Many times though ambulances were going back and forth carrying wounded. As we left, police were pressing forward in teams of a hundred riot cops, and last I saw from several streets up a hill was about 25 cops corner a protestor and repeatedly beat them for five minutes before dragging them away.

Back in the indymedia, we received word that there have been two deaths now confirmed. Cause of death suspected by being hit by charging police vans, and one person shot as well. While here, a person being interviewed described how she was taking photos and then attacked by seven police who dragged her behind a white van and beat her while others destroyed her film and batteries.

As I'm finishing, helicopters are becoming a constant presence overhead, and we hear that many protestors may have started heading back to carlini stadium.

July 21st... Riot aftermath impressions... My eyes are tired. They've been stinging at many points in the day. To walk downtown, one immediately picks up the scent of tear gas. Nothing new I suppose.

Walking downtown after the battle had subsided was kind of surreal. Coming down the stairs onto Corso Italia, was a mass of litter, broken glass, overturned burned out cars, and two blocks of banks and travel agents totally smashed and burned out. We came down on rumours that there was food being given out in the convergence space (after a day of not eating and all the shops closed), but were immediately distracted.

Everyone seemed to be walking around in a daze and just taking it all in, most unaware that conflicts and marches were still happening in other areas. Many of the locals were out on the streets and checking out the burned ruins. People were picking at a melted/smashed banking machine, curious to see what one looks like from the inside.

Contents of bank files and drawers were scattered about with the ashes, photocopiers were melted, sleek cars were black and crushed with odd assorted flags and garbage protruding from them.

In a weird way, it seemed as if everyone was totally fascinated and unable to speak. No one was really condemning it or shaking their heads. It was more like a bewilderment and curiosity. It's not often that one gets to see what lies behind the sleek machines and walls that run our lives.

It was kinda like seeing something you've been taught to respect and fear, become nothing but flimsy garbage. Not even a security guard, cop, or fireman around to keep people away. Feels really artsy or something saying it but it was kinda like a caged animal having their cage fall away, and not really understanding what to do next. Hard to describe I guess.

I saw a family walking down one of the streets picking things up and putting them in bags. The young girl was collecting gas shells. The boy had picked up several pieces of makeshift armour and bits of a flag. A few cars and motorcycles were beginning to return to the streets, casually driving around dumpsters and car wrecks.

Within a few more hours, fire engines and cleaning crews began showing up and returning the city to 'normal'. Meanwhile, just on the other side of the fence in the convergence space, big parties were starting up. Bonfires in the parking lot, drum circles, and lots of people getting drunk at the GSF bars.

I've returned to Indymedia now to find that there have been several incidents of arrests and harassment by police showing up out of nowhere and targeting people on the street. Occasionally a noise happens, someone runs, or silence falls in here and everything gets tense for a second. Paranoia is all around, but things have been so overwhelming at times that there's really not much room for constant paranoia, and the rest of the time, things are pretty mellow.

Some further thoughts on the day... I'm solidifying my negative opinion about the organisers of the GSF. Their control checks for 'passes' into certain zones, like the building the Independent Media Centre is in, are very harsh at times, bordering on hostility.

I have several times been physically stopped from entering a building until I could pull a pass out of my shirt. In times of stress and danger, I can always get in, but many who come have to face a barrage of questions, and I have even seen some-one having to justify why they need medical treatment.

To make matters worse, I have heard from a friend who spoke with an organ-iser, that the police had told the GSF not to allow any demonstrators like black block or Tute Bianche, and they would not attack the GSF spaces. The GSF complied as much as it could, but still got attacked just as much. So much for solidarity, and the rule that no cop ever keeps their word. I am happy that neither the GSF or other organisations have publically denounced any other group but rather focused on the idea that there were many provocateurs.

I was there when the carabinieri raided the IndyMedia Centre and the Diaz school, in Genoa, at the end of the protest against the G8 meeting. We heard the shouts and screams, couldn't get out the door, ran upstairs and hid, fearing for our lives. Eventually the cops found us, but we were the lucky ones. A Member of Parlia-ment was in our building; lawyers and media arrived. There was some obscure Ital-ian legal reason why the police could be deterred. They withdrew.

But nothing could save our friends across the street, at the school where people were sleeping and where another section of the Independent Media where located. The police entered: the media and the politicians were kept out. And they beat people. They beat people who had been sleeping, who held up their hands in a gesture of innocence and cried out, "Pacifisti! Pacifisti!"

They beat the men and the women. They broke bones, smashed teeth, shat-tered skulls. They left blood on the walls, on the windows, a pool of it in every spot where people had been sleeping. When they had finished their work, they brought in the ambulances.

All night long we watched from across the street as the stretchers were carried out, as people were taken to the jail ward of the hospital, or simply to jail. And in the jail, many of them were tortured again, in rooms with pictures of Mussolini on the wall.

This really happened. Not back in the nineteen thirties, but on the night of July 21 and the morning of July 22, 2001. Not in some third world country, but in Italy: prosperous, civilized, sunny Italy. And most of the victims are still in the hospital or in jail, as I write this four days later.

I can't adequately describe the shock and the horror of that night. But as terri-fying as it was to live through it, what is more frightening still are its implications:

✪ That the police could carry out such a brutal act openly, in the face of lawyers, politicians and the media means that they do not expect to be held accountable for their actions. Which means that they had support from higher up, from more power-ful politicians. According to a report published in *La Repubblica* from a policeman who took part in the raid, when the more democratic factions within the police complained that the Constitution was being violated, they were told, "We don't have anything to be worried about, we're covered."

✪ That those politicians also do not expect to be condemned or driven from office means that they too have support from higher up, ultimately, from Berlusconi, Italy's Prime Minister, himself.

✪ That they could beat, torture, and falsely arrest Italians means that they do

not expect to be held accountable by their own people.

✪ That they could beat, torture and imprison internationals shows that they do not expect to be held accountable by the international community. And indeed, who is going to hold them accountable? George Bush, the unelected, unmandated heir of a coup? Sweden, which just used live ammunition on protestors? Canada, builders of the Wall of Shame?

✪ That Berlusconi could support such acts means that he must be certain of support from other international powers, and that these overtly fascist actions are linked to the growing international escalation of repression against protestors.

✪ That the Italian government used tactics learned from Quebec: the wall, the massive use of tear gas, and that the RCMP had observers in Genoa in preparation for next year's meeting in Calgary, means that police repression is also a global network. As we learn from each action, so do they.

✪ That the Italian government are now targeting the organisers of the Genoa Social Forum shows where their agenda was heading all along: the discrediting of the anti-globalisation network, the discouraging of peaceful and legal protest as well as direct action. The leader of the Forum has lost his job. Others are fearing for their freedom and safety.

>> THREE

life during wartime

by JOHN HUGHES

I was on the last plane into Genoa before the airport shut down to all traffic not carrying world leaders and their bodyguards. At Stansted Special Branch had a little booth set up at which they had asked everybody "What's the purpose of your trip?", logging the data into the Schengen Information System, before handing passports back with a false smile and "Have a nice trip!".

Cruising into the downtown area it was swiftly apparent that the city had been cleared for battle. In the maze of medieval lanes that makes up its heart a deathly silence reigned. Almost every shop and business had closed, shutters drawn tightly down, and the residents had disappeared.

A 15 foot high metal fence welded into the ground protected the vast Zona Rossa, in which the G8 were to meet. This Red Zone—ominously in the shape of a gun when you looked at it on the map, the barrel pointing down the main street, the magazine jutting out to the hills, and the trigger guard and stock around the port—cut the city in half, making it extremely difficult for protestors to move around the perimeter. There were almost 20,000 police drawn from every force imaginable—amongst them the Forestry Police in green guarding the Via XX Septembre, the national Polizia in blue, Customs men—the Guardia di Finanza—and the notorious paramilitary Carabinieri, a force historically recruited from poor rural people of the South and used to smash the urban workers of the North. With them were armoured Land Rovers and personnel carriers (APCs) some sporting teargas guns on top, and three helicopters—one more than the Met could field last Mayday. And with another difference from our own boys in blue—this lot were all armed.

I was able to find a vantage point from where, through my binoculars, I could

see small clusters of security men, carabinieri and coastguards lounging at their posts in the Porto Antico, chatting and soaking up the sun while on the quayside the waiters laid the tables that awaited the appointed representatives of the New World Order.

The only other people allowed inside this fortified zone were residents in possession of a police pass and ID who were checked against a list if they dared to leave and sought re-entry. This was life in wartime. Talking about civil rights in Genoa was like talking about rope in the house of a hanged man.

Yet little did we know that even the Geneva Convention would later be abandoned by the Italian State.

The airport shut down, so did the two train stations. The motorways , borders and ports were guarded. A bomb went off at the police HQ, one carabinieri injured in a provocation almost certainly set up by the security services as a warning that a return to the 'Strategy of Tension' of the 1970s would be re-launched if the demonstrations got out of hand.

To say that the atmosphere was tense would be more than an understatement.

But Wednesday night we all made the best of it—a fabulous concert by the sea for the first 15,000 of us with a cooling breeze blowing, beer flowing, dope smoking, and a big red flag of Che Guevara waving. The Convergence Centre was in an excellent location, near to the centre and situated so that the sea-breeze would blow any tear-gas away inland. It was also well provided with cheap food and drink and tables and benches to seat hundreds. But the information provided by the Genoa Social Forum—the GSF—was poor. The map was outdated and inaccurate so we drew our own based on one obtained sneakily from the local police—it was vital to know exactly which streets were blocked and where the Red Zone was. More seriously we found out later that whenever things were kicking off the GSF were unable to say what was happening or to do any more than tell people not to leave the Centre.

The Thursday demo for the rights of migrants passed of peacefully. A very short skirmish with the police was quickly calmed down, people accepting that they might as well save themselves for tomorrow—the day of 'Actions'. And we were still only 50,000—we really needed at least four times that number to make an impact and were worried about people not getting through.

Friday morning we decided to head off in a clockwise circuit and do a tour of the different actions. We had our own camera, binoculars, masks, lemons and water and made the sensible decision to leave swiss army knives at the place we were staying. We decided to carry ID so as not to give the cops an excuse to arrest us if stopped, and wrote lawyers' numbers over our bodies at strategic locations. Some of us had waterproofs, others (showing some foresight) a sandwich. We left our copy of the European Convention on Human Rights behind agreeing that a lemon would be more useful.

First of all we found a small sit-down protest at one of the gates to the Red Zone. Outside, in a double line, the Polizia were already in full riot gear, a small unit about 20 strong, but with teargas guns at the ready. As a couple of dozen veteran protestors struck up a rendition of 'We shall overcome' we decided to head off to find some action. Hard to believe that anything was going to happen here.

The tunnel was blocked so we trudged up the hill and then round to Piazza Cortona where a large procession had made its way down the hill. Again the protestors faced a small squad of Polizia outside the fence. The moustachioed grey-haired cop in charge good humouredly allowed the women's section down to the fence where they tied ribbons and such like, so long as they came back again. Lots of singing, a samba band, a noisy but peaceful throng. They were not going to breach the Red Zone and did not intend to.

We headed off to the Tute Bianche march that by our reckoning should have left the Carlini Stadium for their announced assault on the Red Zone at its strongest point—the Via XX Septembre behind the huge square in front of the main railway station. Why they should choose this location seemed suicidal. Why they should also announce beforehand precisely where they were going to attack seemed incomprehensible. Unless they simply wanted to fail. It was obvious there was no chance of success here. This assessment became even more obvious when we saw that the cops had placed dozens of lorry-sized containers all round the square outside the Red Zone—something they had not done elsewhere. We now had to make a long detour north around the station, and as we were doing so we later learned that the carabinieri had attacked the march as it had come down the hill from Carlini, very close to the spot at which Carlo Giuliani was later shot.

The attack was clearly pre-planned and designed to make things kick off well away from the Red Zone. The police pretty much gave free reign to anyone caring to loot and burn their way along some of these streets so long as they stayed a step ahead. The firemen were given no police protection at all and turned up to deal with a burning wreck only after the direct action brigade had moved on. Barricades had been thrown up at several locations with boarding removed from the banks which were then trashed and the cash-point machines ripped out of the wall. Windows were smashed, some torn away completely and the offices inside wrecked, a few set on fire. A couple of shops were looted a little bit, but not seriously—nobody could really be bothered. Graffiti, mostly in English, completed the artwork.

Just as we emerged from under the railway bridge the police fired off a barrage of tear-gas grenades, and we ran for cover, masking up with a hurried application of lemon juice. The police did not pursue, but we could see them in the distance attacking the front of the Tute Bianche march at the bottom of the long road down from the Stadium where it joins Corso Torino. And we experienced our first whiff of tear-gas, an acrid smell that really gets the adrenalin going!

Small groups were making their way round to a footbridge further up over the railway. Here we could look down the length of the march, but could make out very little at the front due to the clouds of white tear-gas obscuring our vision. We were told that although people at the front were still trying to fight off the police, the march was heading back to Carlini. This seemed bizarre as there were streets open to the south where people could have moved around the flank of the police and tried to join up with other groups. So that's what we tried to do.

Incredibly we walked right through a loose and lazy police line on Corso Torino and found ourselves watching the police being well and truly hammered by a hardy group of stone-throwers. At least a couple of police were carried away unconscious

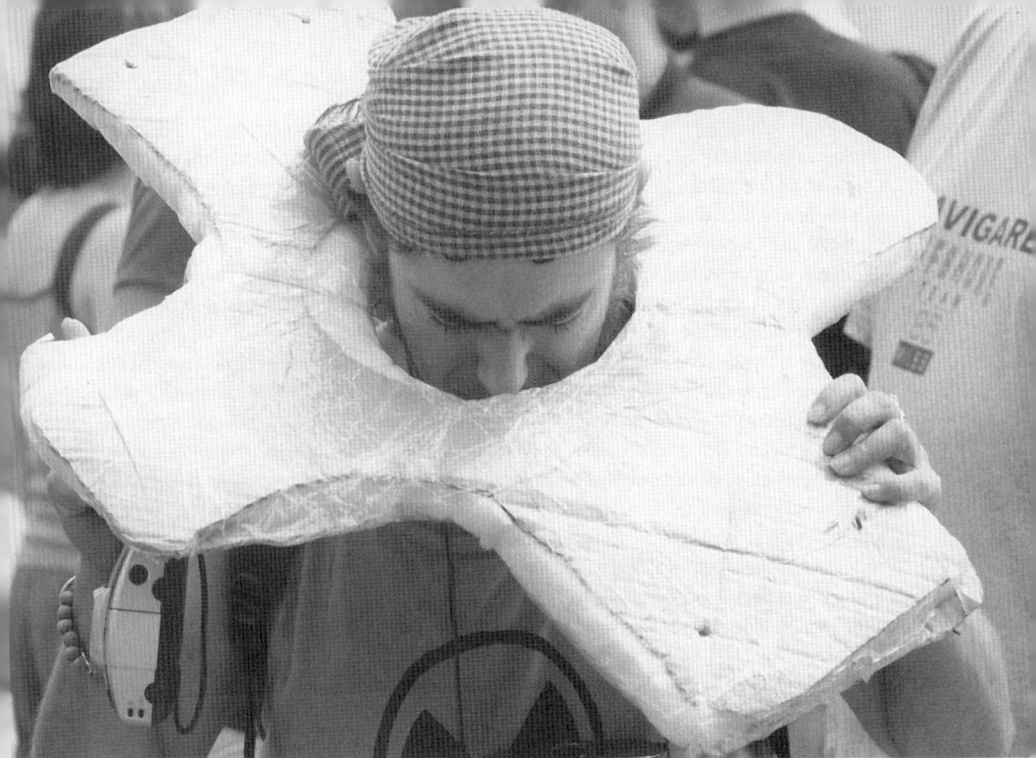

by their colleagues, and the thin blue line looked about to give at one point until they were saved by a massive volley of tear-gas and a mass charge by supporting units that retook the barricade. Nobody however appeared to have been arrested. One cop ran forward with a rifle and fired a huge grenade from it. The barricade itself was made up mainly of large 4-wheeled green rubbish bins and a home-made thick plastic shield welded to an iron frame on two wheels, resembling a mediaeval pavise— part of Tute Bianche's non-violent equipment that was quite impressive. And who were the protestors fighting the police at this point? They weren't the Black Block as far as we could see, they were just—well, whoever had the courage to go down the front. Helmets, goggles and bits of rubber armour were in evidence.

This stretch of Corso Torino near the railway bridge was where the Carabinieri van was caught and burnt. It was the area that saw the main confrontation between police and demonstrators, and was close to where Carlo Giuliani was later shot. For the State it was useful to focus the direct confrontation well away from the Red Zone. Of course it was also useful to those anti-capitalists who were able to smash up banks with impunity. But in truth only small numbers of people, no more than a few hundred, were really involved in direct action at any point, and they seemed a diverse group, many just reacting to the situation of being tear-gassed and seeing people beaten up and fighting back. Ideology was in my view less of a motivation.

Nearby we witnessed photographers being severely beaten up by a group of four plain-clothes police with short truncheons in full view of the nearby riot cops. They obviously had licence to do what they wanted. There was a rumour later that a carabinieri had dropped his wallet which was picked up by a protestor and found to contain a picture of Mussolini. The hard kernel of overt fascists has always been at the heart of the Italian State. The day before we had also seen gangs of cops dressed as demonstrators waiting to infiltrate the crowd. It's not clear what they got up to.

At the Genoa Social Forum later we first heard the news via a mobile call of the death of Carlo Giuliani. No announcement was made by the GSF. It was a shock more than a surprise. Carlo was in my view fairly typical of those prepared to confront the police, a local kid, unaffiliated to either the Black Block or the White Overalls, living an anarchic lifestyle, hanging out at the squatted Pinelli Social Centre. He wasn't well prepared, just with a balaclava, no helmet or armour. And he was in the wrong place at the wrong time. The carabinieri drove at the protestors in two armoured Land Rovers but went too far without infantry support. They were in a square with five exits but one vehicle obviously didn't want to scratch its paintwork by ramming the wheelie-bin out of the way. It was attacked, the cop at the back began waving his gun around, deliberately pointing it at different people. Some saw it and retreated. Some didn't. Carlo walked across the back of the van and picked up a red fire extinguisher lying on the ground. He turned and advanced on the van and was shot in the head. It was no accident and the cop was under no serious threat, but he shot to kill. He was a 21 year old conscript, a puppet of the regime. The driver reversed over Carlo's body, stopped over it as people screamed, then drove forward again, over the body for a second time. The carabinieri advanced shooting tear-gas, one grenade hitting the body. The blood pumped out of Carlo's head like running water. Someone tried to give medical assistance but was chased off by the police. One lone demonstrator stood his ground on the church steps shouting 'Assassini!' He was chased away by police with batons drawn.

In other parts of the city, protestors had reached the Red Zone, but found themselves opposed by watercannon with the water containing CN gas, a variant of CS. A fluffy demo at the top of the road down to Piazza Corvetto was attacked by riot police without reason, tear-gas being shot into the middle of the unsuspecting crowd. Some said they were chasing the ubiquitous members of the Black Block. Later I was worried that there would be attacks on people by the police during the night, either at the GSF or on the streets. I was wrong. Maybe it would be a quiet day tomorrow, I looked forward to a strong, sad, angry demonstration with people wearing black armbands.

Saturday it dawned hot and sunny. A perfect day for a demo. We joined on the long coast road that wound down from the East to the GSF. A huge demo, 300,000 some said. We waited until we saw a sensible looking group—mainly young with a rope round them carrying masks, goggles and stuff you might need in an emergency. And a big banner reading 'Assassini'. We only got a couple of hundred yards before the whole march stopped. We were in the middle, and soon learnt there was trouble upfront. We were advised by the GSF to stay where we were. So we went down the front.

Impossible to see what was happening at the front, just clouds of tear-gas. But we didn't need to wait long as the front came to us! The cops started lobbing tear-gas right into the middle of a completely passive demonstration, people shouting 'bastardi' in anger and anticipation. We watched as the grenades came gracefully arcing through the clear blue sky straight towards us. The coughing and sputtering started. Thankfully I had water and lemon. Within minutes as people retreated back up the hill I found myself in the front line facing a horde of riot cops, armoured personnel carriers and vans sporting tear-gas guns on top. Hardly anybody was bothering to throw anything at the police at this point although there had been a bit of a riot earlier. Cars and banks were burning.

Next thing the police and tanks were moving forward and it was time to get out of there. And it wasn't easy with 50,000 people behind me. It could have been very nasty but a few hundred of us managed to escape over onto the beach. The police didn't pursue which was lucky for us because most people getting caught were getting beaten severely. Offshore the forces of order had no less than 40 different boats and inflatables, fortunately they didn't attack. But we heard that tear-gas was dropped by some of the three helicopters. Whatever had happened before, this was an utterly unprovoked attack on a peaceful demonstration. The trashing went on again up the Corso Torino. The march was split in three, about half or more making it to the rally point. The police didn't even let up the day after killing someone. And later it was going to get a lot worse.

The fence round the Zona Rossa came down just after midnight at Sunday. We walked in and looked around. Gangs of cops and their girlfriends in designer clothes hung out in the bars. It was like a fascist convention. The yuppified Porto Antico was perfect for the G8, boring, sterile designer dockland, superficial with no substance.

Our group got ready to head home—to England, Finland, Holland, Ancona, some moving on to the next gathering of free spirits. One of the best things had been simply spending five days in Genoa living politics, meeting people, discussing ideas, just being there, smelling the tear-gas, feeling the adrenalin, watching the banks burn, being part of a militant and huge gathering. And feeling the shock of Carlo's death, the anger at the fascist behaviour of the police, the relief at getting away without being nicked. And lastly a feeling that we are at the centre of what is rising, not at the fringe of what is dying.

being black block

by K

After Genoa, the black block has been attacked by everyone at a variety of levels. Some accuse the black block of being primarily responsible for the violence in Genoa, others speak of police infiltrators, other accuse it for attacking other demonstrators and others for smashing up things that are not 'legitimate targets'.

Firstly, it needs to remain clear that the black block in Genoa was *not* a unified block, nor a political organisation or anything of that sort which would make these accusations more realistic. The black block is primarily a tactic and, as we understood in Genoa, a dress code. Nothing more. The people who claim that the black block is an organisation are the cops. The fact that the black block attracts those who choose a confrontational attitude towards the cops and property is the only thing that can be said to unify it. But this is not a clear enough distinction: for example the Tute Bianche as well, in their own fucked-up ways, adopt a confrontational relation to the cops. And not everyone outside the black block feels very strongly about property either.

Secondly, the black block is not responsible for the cops' violence against everyone in Genoa. Whoever thinks in those terms should better stay home and watch TV because such an attitude is not only dangerous but shows a complete lack of understanding of the real world.

Thirdly, in terms of police infiltrators. We do not know whether there were cops amongst us in Genoa. Maybe there were, but what does that mean? What difference does it make whether out of a few thousand people willing to attack the riot police and to destroy property some of them are cops? This a matter of concern for those within the black block, as a matter of our security, since cops amongst us might mean that some of us get arrested more easily because we have been identified or followed by cops (we were told this happened in Barcelona during the anti-IMF/World Bank demos). Apart from that it does not make a fucking difference.

What are the political gains, on the other hand, that can be made by those who accuse the block of being infiltrated by cops? It is not by chance, for example, that the main people who came up with their ground-breaking stories of the type 'I saw black block people coming from inside police vans' (like that scumbag Agnoletto's brother) were either from the Genoa Social Forum or some Italian Communist MPs—their political ideology necessitates the separation of people into 'bad' and 'good', and it is historically the case that those who do not follow their lead are easily dismissed as cops. And isn't it curious how some Tute Bianche accuse the black block of having cops at its ranks when they themselves had made a special deal with the cops, for which they were complaining in Italian mainstream newspapers on the Saturday 21st July because the police didn't keep? The Genoa Social Forum produced a photo which supposedly proves the point that there were police infiltrators in the black block. This picture however only proves the stupidity of the Social Forum. It shows some cops in uniform and others in normal clothes who are wearing scarves. Do you really have to be a fucking genius to understand that some cops will be wearing scarves to protect themselves from the tons of tear gas they threw, especially if they do not have gas masks? How does that stupid fact prove that some cops were in the black block?

A further claim is that those cops are there to start smashing things in order to get everyone involved. This is so stupid that any 5-year old can easily dismiss. Does anyone really think that anyone in the black block needs infiltrators in order to start smashing things up or to attack cops?

In terms of the black block attacking other demonstrators this is again a dangerous rumour that is being spread by idiots like Agnoletto's brother. The black block did not engage into attacking other demonstrators. If some fights broke out with other demonstrators they were not always provoked by the black block (we were attacked by Cobas people, for example, though we forgive them because they were pretty frustrated from the fact that the black block fucked up their demonstration and their attitude generally those days was fucking excellent—anyone who stayed at the psychiatric hospital knows what we mean), and even if they were these concern individuals within the black block and not everyone who was wearing black. So the black block attacked other demonstrators as much as other demonstrators attacked the black block. There was no fucking plan to attack other demonstrators.

The fact that certain of the targets of the black block in Genoa are not considered 'legitimate' by everyone (even by other black blockers), is an issue that is unrelated to police infiltrators. Even if there were cops who were smashing proletarian shops it does not matter, because the point is that there are people among the black block who do not think that this is a problem and who got engaged in such actions themselves.

The idea that certain targets are legitimate whereas others aren't betrays a problematic part of the ideology of anti-globalisation. Capitalism is not just the big corporations, but a social relation which manifests itself as much in the big corp-

orate stores and symbols (e.g. McDonalds) as in the small corner shops. It has to do with the fact that wherever we go, whether in a Marks & Spencer or the family corner shop, we are confronted with a world of commodities that only money can buy. The destruction of capitalism does not mean that the world will be transformed into environmentally friendly, organic-selling local shops, but that exchange and money in their totality will disappear.

Having said that, it is also clear that the destruction of capitalism does not depend on the amount of windows that we can smash. But to say that does not mean to condemn actions that took place in Genoa (or take place in other parts of the world) as misled. We were not in Genoa to destroy capitalism, so that kind of criticism misses the point. What happened in Genoa was a generalised riot, not an anti-capitalist insurrection (those who do not understand the difference should better go home to join the other idiots from above).

During riots, and the chaotic situation that these bring about, a lot of things can go wrong and it is fair enough to say that certain targets should be avoided. But again this is mostly a strategic issue and not a political or moral one. If the cops attack us with everything they have and we need to build barricades, we will make them with whatever is immediately available. We will not sit around in the street trying to figure out whether this or that car are bourgeois or proletarian. And if a small shop is attacked in order to get water and drinks for the rioters then so be it. Now if people insist on attacking phone boxes or traffic lights (one explanation for that was that it would create traffic jams in the following days) or other seemingly stupid targets, then people should ask them to stop. But we are not going to go around riots trying

to get people to behave, let alone if the argument is that some companies are capitalist whereas others aren't.

If the black block deserves criticism for some of its actions in Genoa, these are of a different kind: for example, it is in fact a huge problem for people to smash telephone boxes or traffic lights when we are being charged by armoured cars and riot cops and we need to build strong barricades to hold them back. But again this is a problem of strategy and tactics, not a moral issue. As we said before, the black block in Genoa consisted of a wide variety of people whose only common ground was a desire to attack cops and property. This situation means that there were a lot of idiots amongst us who do not find it in themselves to prioritise certain things to others. It is one thing, however, to say that there are idiots among us and quite another to say that there were cops who 'orchestrated' our actions.

Another point of criticism of the black block concerns the fact that on Friday it started attacking cops and property as soon as the demo started, a fact which meant that the black block was split into two parts (one went north, the other south with the Cobas). This was as much a result of stupidity (given that when people from the black block itself expressed the desire to keep our strengths for later and not waste all our petrol bombs in the first twenty minutes they were ignored) as well as a result of bad co-ordination. The black block did not manage to meet and discuss constructively the days before Friday so no-one really knew what was going on. Given that the majority of the black block however clearly expressed to those who started smashing things and attacking the cops that this was not the moment for it, these actions cannot be justified.

This brings us to a crucial point about Genoa. The black block generally failed in (or was forced to abandon the idea of) attacking the cops in a good way. And this could be perhaps the only 'accusation' that can be brought against the black block (although it is not really an accusation since in many respects we were forced to do this, it was not simply a matter of choice after a certain point). Contrary to popular myths, the most hardcore riots that took place in Genoa were those near Brignole station, and it was in these riots that Carlo Giuliani was killed. These riots were not made by either the black block or the Tute Bianche. Instead, a wide variety of people took part in these—some were Tute Bianche who got fucked off with their usual staged-confrontation and abandoned their formations, others were people who left the black block because vandalism became too ritualistic, others were members of reformist organisations and parties who got outraged by the police violence and chose to respond in the best possible way etc etc.

In a sense, this was one of the most important events about Genoa, and no group or organisation (be it the black block or Tute Bianche or whoever) can take the credit for. It was the moment when people chose to abandon pre-determined tactics and sterile organisations and to attack the cops in any way possible. This resulted in the most organised riot that we saw in Genoa those days: there were people at the front with shields, gloves and masks (either Tute Bianche people or others who took up their equipment) taking care of the tear gas, and behind them loads of people with rocks and some petrol bombs. These were the people who chased off the cops for about one kilometre, who formed barricades which were carried forward every time the cops retreated, these were the people that forced the cops to pull their guns in order to stop them and who needed armoured cars charging at them at 60 kilometres an hour to get them to retreat.

This is a fact that many people have an interest in concealing, either because they do not want to admit that their members broke the party line or because they want to show off about being in the best riot in some other place in Genoa. We, on the other hand, don't give a fuck because we have nothing to protect or to show off.

genoa genoa

by JOSE

I arrived in Genoa with two friends the Tuesday before the demonstrations. The first one was going to be on Thursday, but we had some information about controls in the borders and in the airport, and we were afraid about not getting into the city. With the help of a comrade from Alessandria, a city near to Genoa, we got into the fortress without any problems. I say fortress because that is what they had turned the city into for the occasion of the G8 conference. 25,000 members of the repression forces protected the Red Zone, an area that covered the centre of the city where there were going to be the conferences. While we looked for the meeting point, we could check the magnitude of the force at the police disposition, that included antiriot police in dozens on every corner, metal walls, helicopters, light tanks and the army in the streets with automatic guns.

The organisation of the conference by the Genoa Social Forum was very good, the meeting point was an enormous space with a canteen, information tables about places to sleep and volunteers, and a stage where on Wednesday was playing Manu Chao. Another place that we met up was a park used like a camp site, where a part of the Black Block were and where we slept the most part of the days, the Indymedia Centre, Diaz school or the Stadium of the Tute Bianche.

The Thursday demonstration that crowded together all the groups that were in the anti-globalisation movement, demanded the rights for the immigrants and happened without conflicts with between 50,000 and 100,000 demonstrators. The Friday was the day to break the Red Zone, and of course the G8 meetings. The different groups had gone to try in separated blocks with different tactics. The pacifist groups went under the name of Pink March, in another place Rifundazione Com-

unista went with other groups like Attac, the ecologists were in another block, there was a base union called 'Cobas', and of course the Black Block. The Black Block went out of the camp site early in the morning, around 11:30. The spatial and time proximity with the Cobas demonstration made unavoidable the mixing between both demonstrations in Corso Torino. Early, much too early were broken the first windows of the first bank, after that the police attacked the demonstration of thousands and thousands of people, with tear-gas and sticks. Some people of the Cobas, and the Black Block, tried to calm the people but the confrontation with the police began and didn't stop. The Black Block confronted the police with stones and bottles, but it was unavoidable that we moved back to join with the Cobas in the direction of the centre of the city. After that the police repression didn't stop all the day.

The members of the Black Block, now joined to young people of the Cobas, began to make barricades to stop the police. When we arrived to the square the police oppression was so big that the demonstration was split up in different groups. I don't know what happened with the other ones, but after that the demonstration took the form of a riot in all the area to the east of the Red Zone. The different Blocks was mixed,—in the one that I was in, the majority was Black Blockers but a lot of Italian anarchists and communists too. The systematic destruction of banks, temporary job agencies and estate agents followed in the afternoon, also dealing with the police attacks and building the barricades.

In one moment of the demonstration, after crossing the river in the direction of the centre, I saw some members of the Black Block attacking a supposed secret policeman. While I walked over to them, another policeman dressed as a rioter took out a gun and shot three times in the air, and two other secret police turned up on motorbikes and took them away. The infiltrated police was a fact, but not only in the Black Block, it is impossible to control that in a mass demonstration.

The march continued. Some demonstrators with more experience tried to limit the aggression to the banks and estate agents, but more than one car was burnt in a barricade when we protected ourselves against the police, and a police car was burned. Outside the jail there was a strong confrontation with the police and people threw some molotovs, this was the only place where I saw the police had to move back. Anyway the jail was empty for the occasion. Between three and four o'clock in the afternoon, we arrived to a square where were some demonstrators of the Pink March, at that time the Black Block demonstration was half broken and dispersed in the constant fights and we were around seven hundred. After we rested some minutes in the square, without any warning the tear gas fell again and the police attacked both demonstrations with sticks, without distinction between us and the pacifists that were separated from us. I think we had part of the responsibility for that but we didn't intend it in any way.

Escaping from the police that were coming behind us, we arrived near to the Red Zone. In front of us was a wall with few hundred policemen with shields and sticks, supported by light tanks, and throwing tear gas at us. The people was preparing to break the human wall with wheel rubbish bins, bottles, stones, and some molotovs. The confrontation looked unavoidable, but a group of pacifists, with white hands, went on their knees between us and the police facing us to obstruct the fight. After that it was easy for the police to disperse us with tear gas, leaving us in a more and more reduced group when we regrouped again. We tried in another street, but in all the streets that went to the centre we found similar blockades waiting for us with tear gas and sticks. When I realised we were a few people, less than a hundred I thought it was useless to continue. It was around six in the afternoon, but in another places the riots continued to eight o'clock. Little by little the police were eliminating the resistance, less and less people, and more and more isolated. When I arrived to the meeting point, around half past eight in the night, there was chaos. The people spoke about some dead people, hundreds injured and arrested, and the organisers recommended we didn't go into the street in little groups, as they were afraid of the police reprisals.

The Saturday was another demonstration of all the groups joined. In the minds of everybody was Carlo Giuliani. 300,000 demonstrators took the streets of the city reclaiming justice.

The hate was strong and a little while after the beginning of the demonstration, a big group of demonstrators, Italians in the most part, went directly against the police. In the square of Kennedy the confrontations began at half past three in the afternoon, all the banks in the place were burned and a lot of cars, the people threw bottles at the police and were throwing back the tear gas canisters, that the police were using like projectiles against the rioters. That day a big cloud of gas covered Genoa. A lot of people in bad condition from the gas were helped in the social centres. Everybody was scared to go the hospitals, the next day all the demonstrators injured in the hospitals were arrested, some of them without having medical attention. We had news of police attacks in all the parts of the demonstration, a lot of people injured, attacks against the medical services and journalists... Around seven o'clock the police had the situation completely under control.

That night we went to the Briganole station, that looked like a refugee camp. It was there, waiting for the train where we realised that the Indymedia centre and the school were being attacked.

> > S I X

being busy

by ANONYMOUS

It became obvious when I got to Genoa that, like in Prague, the protests had a fair degree of mainstream acceptance. The convergence centre had a huge marquee that must have cost a fortune to hire and a big stage with a giant PA and lighting rig, together with lots of over-priced hot-dog vendors and a bar. It was like being at the Glastonbury Festival. These people obviously had some money.

And indeed this turned out to be true. The GSF (Genoa Social Forum), which was the official organising body for the protests, was a coalition of about 700 different NGOs (Non-Governmental Organisations—i.e. charities, pressure groups etc.) and other 'civil society organisations'. It enjoyed a fair degree of mainstream support, including that of the lefty Genoa city council, which had let them have the space for our convergence centre, as well as a school building for their media centre and several sports stadiums for all the demonstrators to stay in. Apparently this even extended to the police as well. Someone told me that the Polizia Municipale, under the control of the city council, were more sympathetic to us than the Carabinieri or any of the other nationally-controlled types of police present in Genoa. So we even had lefty police!

THE LEFT IN ITALY

This is a situation hard to imagine in present-day Britain. In Italy the left and institutionalised social democracy exists to a far greater extent than in Britain. The closest we've got is 'Red' Ken Livingstone and some local lefty councils. If you imagine a return to the glory days of the 1980s when Ken was at the height of his power as head of the GLC, Militant ran Liverpool and loony left councils were declaring nuclear-

free zones across the country then you're getting closer to what it's like in Italy. Even though Ken has on occasion cautiously expressed his support for anti-globalisation protesters, still it's difficult to imagine in this country a city council supporting the anti-G8 protests, or those protests having the involvement of major unions.

So in Italy the left is still alive and well (and far more Leninist than it ever was in Britain) and the whole political culture of the left is far more widespread and ingrained than in Britain. On the immigrants march on the Thursday in Genoa the band struck up the *Internationale* and everyone (except the Brits and the Americans) knew all the words, and were singing along with clenched fists in the air. They proceeded to play a whole bunch of other classic left songs which everyone also seemed to know all the words to. Another thing that you can't imagine in Britain.

The reason for these differences is partly because the whole inter-generational culture of the labour movement which did exist in this country has been destroyed over the last 20 years or so of Thatcherism. With the decimation of heavy industry and the restructuring of the economy most of the old strongholds of the workers' move-ment no longer exist—e.g. mining, shipbuilding, the docks and the nationalised industries. It is partly also because this ingrained leftism was never as strong in Britain as in Italy anyway. The Communist Party has never been a very significant force in British politics, whereas in Italy it has dominated the post-war period, if only by virtue of the fact that no effort was spared to keep it out of power. In Genoa you could see more hammer and sickle flags in one day than you'd see in Britain in the rest of your life. The Communist Party drew much of its prestige in the post-war period from the fact that it was the only organised group to fight the fascists. The partisans of the resistance movement were dominated by the Communists and in Genoa they succeeded in liberating the city from Mussolini's forces without the help of the Americans (this last part being especially important). The memory of the part-isans is obviously still alive and well even among young Italians—whenever a band struck up the partisan song *Bella Ciao* all the Italians went crazy, singing and jump-ing around and punching their fists in the air.

Understanding the power the traditional left still has in Italy will give you some idea of how they managed to get 200,000 people to Genoa (20 times more than were in Prague!). The vast majority of these were Italian and it was the Italian left of parties, unions and various different sorts of Leninists that made up the bulk of the numbers.

THE PLAN

The basic plan broke down like this—Thursday 19th was the day of the immigrants' march for illegal workers and asylum seekers and against 'Fortress Europe' and its policies of exclusion. This was to be entirely peaceful as the immigrants themselves were to be on the march and couldn't risk getting arrested as they would then be sent back to whatever country they had just escaped from, with who knows what consequences. Then Friday 20th was to be the direct action day, when different groups would take all different sorts of action against the G8 summit and the Red Zone protecting it. The idea was, similarly to previous summit protests, that different groups would take different positions around the perimeter of the Red Zone and carry out their various different forms of actions, therefore in theory allowing pacifists to take action along the north edge of the Red Zone, while the black block attacked the eastern edge of the Red Zone, for example. This scheme was supposed to keep everyone happy, because it allows everyone to do their own thing unimpeded by people who want to do something different. How this actually worked out on the day will be seen below. Saturday 21st was planned as the big united march of everyone, including all the parties and the unions and obviously including everyone who was working and couldn't come during the week. This, like Thursday, was supposed to be entirely peaceful and just a straightforward march from point A to point B, with a rally and speakers and no violence.

THE BLACK BLOCK

When foreign anarchists arrived in Genoa they found that the Italian anarchists had not organised anything. Apart from the workers' march, there was no black block meeting point organised for the Friday. In the long run up to the Genoa protests most Italian anarchists seemed to have spent their time denouncing the GSF for being a bunch of liberals and had expended their energy doing this rather than organising anything themselves. Many had decided that the whole thing was completely compromised by liberal reformist ideas and that it was all a waste of time and had basically decided to have nothing to do with it. So when the international anarchists started showing up in the few days prior to the protests, they had to run around trying to organise an anarchist meeting point at the last moment. To the extent that the black block was organised at all, it was organised by international anarchists at the last moment. The main debate was over where the anarchists were going to go on Friday: were we strong enough to have our own meeting point or were we going to latch on to someone else's march and meeting point? After some discussion with some of the other groups participating on the Friday, at which it seemed that no-one wanted the poor old black block, it was eventually decided that we would all meet at the same meeting point as the Cobas (a coalition of grass roots unions), because their politics were in some ways the closest to our own and they also seemed to be up for some action and for trying to get into the Red Zone.

In Europe, it is usually not just the black block which is a block—*everyone* is in blocs. A normal leftie demo on the continent will be composed of all the various parties and unions arranged in blocs, one after the other, each marching in a group behind their banner. It is normal for the anarchists (whether by choice or compulsion is unclear) to bring up the rear of the march, forming a black block at the end of the demo, often trashing things along the route of the march or fighting the police. As the concept of the black block has travelled around the world, to Britain and America and elsewhere, it has left behind this original social context that it came from.

Another thing that needs sorting out is the identification of the black block with anarchists. In Genoa on Friday and Saturday there were lots of anarchists who were not in the black block and lots of people in the black block who were not anarchists. Although on the Friday anarchists did organise a pre-arranged meet-up point for the black block, there were many more people engaged in black block-esque street fighting than simply the anarchists. And on the Saturday there was no pre-arranged

plan at all—simply that people who wanted to fight went where the fighting was and people who didn't tried to stay away.

Against some on the left who have tried to present the black block as something uniquely anarchist, even tracing the origins of the black block back to Bakunin's fondness for clandestine plotting and secret cells, and also against those anarchists who have tried to present the black block as something uniquely anarchist, it needs saying that there is nothing uniquely anarchist in the origins of the black block. As far as I understand it, the technique of the black block originated mainly in the 1980s autonomen scene in Northern Europe, which was at least as much anti-imperialist/Leninist as it was anarchist. This was clear to be seen in Genoa as well, for all that the media made much of the 'anarchist' black block, if you look at photos of those engaged in the rioting there are loads of red hammer and sickle flags in amongst the black-clad people, probably more than there are anarchist flags. As an example, I saw people from the PKK (Kurdistan Workers Party) and Basque nationalists in with the black block.

And in response to the various left groups, with their very obvious self-serving agendas, all jostling for the best position in order to exploit the fame of the Genoa protests, it needs to be said that the black block is no sort of organisation, no sort of group. It does not exist outside the demonstration and is united only on that demonstration by some minimal unity of tactics—people who are up for property destruction and for fighting the police. Basically, to cut through all the mythologising bullshit, it's as simple as this—on a big demo like in Genoa, everyone wants to hang out with people who are up for the same thing they are. Even without any prior organisation at all, if a fight starts with the police, people who want to fight the police will move to the front to be a part of it, and those who don't will move in the opposite direction. Therefore, just by default, effective groups will emerge. Given that quite a lot of people have been on a few demos over time, some collective ideas have emerged—masking up being one and trying to wear similar-looking clothing being another. Both for very straightforward practical reasons. That is all the black block is.

Some accuse the black block or those who engage in more militant activity in general of being 'elitist'. This is an absurd distortion. The point of being an elite is that you try an exercise power over other people. The point about the black block is that people simply want the autonomy to be able to express their anger as they see fit. There is nothing elitist in that. Accusing the black block of being a vanguard or an elite when no one ever tries to tell anyone else what to do is ridiculous. In the case of the Leninist party organisations that criticise the black block for this reason, their motives are pretty clear—the mode of organisation they favour is 'democratic centralism'—where everyone would be subjected to some huge democratic process of deciding what would and wouldn't be allowed on demos, a decision, when made by our 'representatives' would then be enforced. Now that really would be elitist.

Despite all of this, there may be a positive side to the way anarchists are always credited with all the most militant activity. So, rather than always complaining about how anarchists get demonised by the media as violent troublemakers, perhaps we should try looking at the positive side to this. When the name of anarchist has become synonymous with the most militant section of the protest movement that gives us a certain advantage. If a larger social struggle does kick off at some point in the future this may put us in a position of having a certain amount of street cred if nothing more. And people attracted to the militancy and hearing that it's all anarchists, may want to learn more about the politics. And it must really annoy the PKK et al. that whenever they engage in militant activity they get called anarchists.

POLICE TACTICS

The Thursday immigrant march went pretty smoothly—it was noisy, musical, colourful and completely non-violent. It was at least half anarchists, a situation that was not to be replicated on any of the following days. At one point where the march turned a corner and passed a line of cops someone threw something at the cops and they were ready to charge into the crowd, but anarchists formed a line between the cops and the crowd to stop this and in order to stop any further violence. Not a scene that you will often see, admittedly, but one that goes to disprove the image of anarchists as simply violent troublemakers and mindless hooligans. People quite clearly recognised that the immigrant march was not the time or the place for any fighting to happen and stopped it from happening.

Friday's direct action day was of course the day that saw the most militant fighting and the most violence. Many anarchists involved in the FAI (like the Italian version of the Anarchist Federation here) had spent a long time organising with a group of workers who were on strike in the west of Genoa to have a march on the Friday that would march from the site of the strike, around the perimeter of the Red Zone. They had promised the workers that there would not be any violence on this march, as some of the workers would have their families present etc. So on the Friday, a fairly substantial section of anarchists did not join the black block but joined the workers' march in the west of the city. Then to the north of the Red Zone was the area where several different pacifist organisations would be holding their actions. The Tute Bianche (White Overalls) groups would be marching directly from their stadium in the east of the city to the Red Zone and attempting the break in on the eastern side. Then the Cobas and the black block were slightly to the south of the Tute Bianche, and other groups, like Globalise Resistance, ATTAC and the Pink and Silver group were marching on the Red Zone from the South side. In actual fact these neat distinctions pretty soon broke down as soon as anything actually kicked off, as the black block were split in half and forced in different directions, the Tute Bianche were repulsed by the police and various other groups all mingled together. Later on in the day you could see Tute Bianche, black block-ers, people from the social centres, Cobas etc. all side by side. And as some of the padded-up Tute Bianche shed their armour and others donned theirs, people rapidly became indistinguishable.

The police strategy for the day seemed to rely mostly on hitting everyone with huge amounts of tear gas almost regardless of who they were or whether they were doing anything. As hardly anyone had proper gas masks this had a large effect. The idea seems to have been to try and disperse the crowds by the use of tear gas and to slowly drive them away from the Red Zone and off into the suburbs of Genoa. People panicked and ran far too easily when the police started firing tear gas and constantly had to be restrained by some individuals calling for them to calm down and not to run. When people in a crowd start running, everyone else starts running too and with a large crowd in a confined area people can get trampled and squashed because everyone is being shoved on by the stampeding masses behind. In this sort of situation the panicking crowd is quite easily more dangerous than the tear gas. And in any case people were picking up the tear gas and throwing it back at the cops, which seemed to work quite well.

The result of these police tactics was that the protests and all the fighting on Friday was basically a large and not particularly organised retreat lasting several hours. We started off relatively close to the centre and to the Red Zone and then as soon as any fighting kicked off, the police fired huge volumes of tear gas and advanced, scattering and dispersing the crowd. Elements of the crowd attempted to slow the retreat and to buy some time by erecting barricades and attacking the police, but by and large the day consisted of the demonstrators being split into smaller and smaller groups and pushed further and further from the town centre and out into the suburbs.

This had several results. It is worth noting that from the beginning almost everything really worth attacking was already sealed away inside the Red Zone, which looked like it had been extended to include the main boulevard of posh shops. Therefore from the outset the demonstrators were only left with the outskirts of town to smash up and as the police advanced and pushed people further away and off into the outlying areas of town the potential targets became more and more mundane (a corner shop, a newspaper kiosk...).

MINDFUL DESTRUCTION

Hence some people's complaints that the black block destroyed a lot of minor property—small shops, ordinary cars and so on. A lot of the time this was the only sort of thing around. Which maybe should have meant that people didn't smash anything at all, and certainly the bank that I saw which had been set on fire underneath a whole set of apartments seemed like a pretty stupid thing to have done (especially considering the locals had been overwhelmingly supportive, giving demonstrators/rioters food and water, allowing them to hide in their houses from the cops, cheering us on, giving us rides etc.). However, sometimes coming under attack from the police, you have to use whatever is to hand. And if you need to use a car or a litter bin to barricade the street with, then so be it. Some of the complaints I heard from some people just seemed to me to be remarkably petty, when people were complaining that phone boxes or bus shelters got destroyed. OK, so they did. And, yes, it's true that these things are not generally used by the rich. But on the other hand it's a *riot*, and riots generally contain a fair amount of chaos and disorder. OK, maybe if everyone was acting with perfect good order and discipline then these things wouldn't have happened, but really in the great scheme of things, does it really matter? For fuck's sake, phone boxes get smashed up every day of the week anyway. Riots have historically proven to be a very effective way for the dispossessed to make their voices heard and to enforce their will—does anyone really imagine that in the French Revolution, or the Peasant's Revolt, or the bread riots of the 19th century or the anti-structural adjustment riots in the Third World today that no random stupid shit happened? Of course it did, and if there's ever going to be any sort of revolution then it will probably involve a whole lot more random chaos and disorder and fucked-up stuff happening, so get used to it.

However, that said, it doesn't mean that we shouldn't try and minimise this and conduct ourselves with as much good order as possible. Which to their credit people were doing. Contrary to the stereotypes of anarchists thugs engaging in mindless and uncontrolled destruction, everything I saw (maybe the burning bank excepted) seemed very soberly done and thoughtful—walking down the Corso Torino in the aftermath of some of the fighting it was completely clear to see—every single bank was smashed to pieces and *nothing* else was. There were also numerous examples of people questioning each other during the fighting about what they were doing and attempting to stop people doing especially stupid things, of the crowd policing itself in a way. Crowds and riots are almost never as 'wild' and 'uncontrolled' as the media would have you believe. Most people involved know very clearly what they are doing and can tell you why.

But there were some people doing fairly silly things during the fighting. One friend of mine said it seemed like rioting by numbers: there were lots of young people there who had maybe been attracted to the protests by coverage of other similar things they had seen on TV, and they were doing what they'd seen on telly—what they thought you were *supposed* to do during riots. So people were building barricades in the streets when there was no need to and then when they were needed to hold the police back, they would be deserted as everyone ran away. Lots of people seemed more keen on smashing things up than on defending the space against the police. And people were smashing up random things that made no sense. On one occasion a group raided a little corner shop and dragged a crate of cola or something into the street and then smashed up all the bottles with hammers.

It is worth noting that the police response to the demonstrators did not seem to be related to who was 'violent' and who was 'peaceful'—they used violence and tear gas and water cannons against everyone—against the pink and silver dancers, against the Trots, against the Tute Bianche and against the black block. This clearly shows the falsity of the idea that militant sections of the crowd 'provoke' the violence of the police and that if only we were all pacifists then the police would leave us alone. It is a ridiculous presumption in a way to believe that we can 'decide' how the police will react to us. We had ensured that we were going to get a violent response by gathering in the streets in such large numbers and announcing our intention to get inside the Red Zone. That is a provocative and confrontational stance to take, whether or not you are throwing molotov cocktails. Then the black block get all the blame for the violence on account of being the only people actually prepared for the violence that the *entire* demonstration has inevitably provoked. The police strategy was clearly to attack everyone equally to punish and scare off the non-violent people on the protests from future participation in these sort of events. The police respond to the level of violence you threaten and to your effectiveness. If you are ineffective but violent, you will probably get a response from the police, if you are ineffective and non-violent then you will probably not get much response from the police, but if you begin to be effective, whether or not you are using violence or not, then you will be met with a violent response. This was true in Seattle and it was true in Genoa.

Some people have complained about how the trashing of the town detracted from the aim of getting inside the Red Zone. This is self-delusion really. Most people made a fairly realistic assessment that we were unlikely to get inside the Red Zone in any large numbers and that if a substantial number of people did manage to breach their defences then the police would probably open fire anyway. After all, the police had known the exact day we would attempt our attack for several months, and giving them that much time to prepare, you are unlikely to be able to get past them. Under these circumstances, trashing the town was potentially the best thing to do. The police were too busy protecting the Red Zone, we had effective control of the streets, and this level of destruction will send out an effective message to the whole world, but especially to any other cities that are thinking of hosting summit meetings that if they do then this is what will happen to their city too. This is making these kinds of summit meetings harder and harder to hold, as *The Guardian* reported: "there is a shortage of cities queuing up to be turned into a war zone".

This is one important thing to remember about Genoa—because it was a G8 summit, all the world's media were there, and the news and the images of the rioting will have been carried back to almost every country in the world. The value of this, especially in much of the Third World is inestimable. Many people in other countries in the world imagine that everyone in the West lives a life of indolent luxury. Remember that *Baywatch* is the most popular TV programme in the world. This is the image that many people across the world have of life in the West. It is very valuable for them to be able to see images of things they are familiar with—poor people fighting the police—taking place in the 'rich' West, leading them to see that the image they have been fed of the Western lifestyle is not all it's cracked up to be and that maybe there are people like them in the West fighting for the same things they are fighting for. The riots in Genoa will send a message of hope to people all over the world that right inside the belly of the beast there are thousands of people who are against the system and are prepared to risk their own life and liberty to fight it.

INFILTRATORS, PROVOCATEURS, FASCISTS AND COPS

So there were quite a few people within the black block who did some stupid things. Well, nothing new there then. Some people have said that the black block split fairly early on and a whole bunch of people left and went off and did their own thing because they got fed up with the stupid shit that some people were doing. Some people have suggested that the black block which was going around doing the more fucked-up anti-social stuff then moved off to the area where the pacifists were and started attacking the police at those points, leading the police to pile in and attack the pacifists. Apparently, this anti-social black block then moved off way away from both the Red Zone and the police and started just randomly destroying ordinary people's property. For these and some other reasons some people have suggested that this more fucked-up segment of the black block was composed of police.

Some Leninist and left-liberal groups have gone further than this and have put about the story that the black block and the police acted together, 'orchestrating' the violence. Apparently, the police allowed the black block to act unhindered and did not stop them or arrest them when they could have done but instead used them by

driving the black block into some other sections of the crowd on purpose to give them a reason to attack the peaceful parts of the demonstration. Now there may or may not have been police infiltrators in the Black Block, I don't know. But I do know for sure that the police did not orchestrate anything with the Black Block as a whole, the Black Block had no 'plan' to work with the police to disrupt the peaceful demonstrators, as some of the paranoid rubbish put about by some of the left-liberal groups would suggest. For one thing this would be impossible as the Black Block had no 'plan' of any sort at all. And as for allowing us to go about 'unhindered'... well, apart from all the tear gas, baton charges, water cannons, tanks being driven at us and being shot at, yes, we were pretty much unhindered...

And while we're on the subject of infiltration, lots of the left-liberal groups who've been accusing the black block of being cops and fascists and of all being infiltrators etc. etc. *ad nauseam* act is if they are somehow magically immune to infiltration themselves. The finest example of this nonsense being *Socialist Worker* claiming that "the Black Block's methods and use of masks opens them up to police infiltration"—how exactly are non-masked-up, non-violent groups any less easy to infiltrate? It is certainly entirely plausible that the cops would infiltrate the black block—that is exactly the sort of thing they would do. But so also would they likewise infiltrate all the other organisations, including all of those now attacking the black block. Indeed is it not just as likely a cop tactic to place cops within the left-liberal organisations to ensure that they denounce the more militant elements of the crowd as it is that the cops would attempt to infiltrate the more militant sections? I'm not saying it's true, I'm just saying it's got about the same likelihood of being true as the black

block being infiltrated by cops and fascists.

Whether or not it actually happened in Genoa, it is certainly entirely possible for the police to infiltrate the black block and to try and antagonise other protesters and the general public against the more militant elements of these protests. So regardless of whether it actually happened in this instance, we need to be aware that it easily *could* happen and we need to develop some mechanisms to guard against this, if possible. Probably the best way of doing this would be by developing better collective solidarity and self-policing—allowing people to challenge others in the crowd who are engaging in counter-productive behaviour.

SATURDAY AND AFTER

After Friday when we had all heard that a guy was shot dead, we were wondering what Saturday was going to be like—would it be really angry as a result or would everyone be scared? As it turned out, Saturday was in many ways a re-run of Friday's rioting, with the difference that there was greater antagonism towards the black block from some of the other demonstrators, some blaming them for the shooting the previous day and also with some accusing them of being cops or fascists. There were probably more people on the streets, but with numbers this large it is in any case almost impossible to estimate whether you're talking about 100,000 or 200,000. Although Saturday was supposed to be peaceful, this had never been agreed to as unanimously as for the Thursday event and it pretty much kicked off immediately. However, groups like the Tute Bianche, which on Friday had been all padded-up for direct action were now picking on people who had any padding and were forming lines to keep the main bulk of the march separate from the people engaged in fighting the police. Most of the people on the march probably did in fact complete the designated route without being caught up in any street fighting, although they might have got gassed a bit. The rioting on Saturday carried on into the evening, culminating late in the night with the police raid on the GSF media centre and the school where many people were staying.

The main bulk of the crowds that had filled the streets on Saturday left very quickly on Sunday. It was amazing how quickly everyone melted away. Partly this was due to fear of a police crackdown, but the dissipating numbers strengthened this process as the more people left town the more vulnerable the remaining few felt. The GSF laid on special buses and trains to whisk people away and out of the area as swiftly as possible.

THE NUMBERS GAME

On demonstrations like these there are two main factors that are constantly argued over—militancy and numbers. One group of people are worried that certain levels of militancy will reduce the numbers on protests, and the others are worried that large numbers mean nothing if no-one does anything. Both points of view have some truth to them. Clearly numbers in themselves mean nothing. If those people are threatening nothing and are so well policed and disciplined that there's no danger of them getting out of hand, then you can have demos as big as you like and it means nothing. Lots of people were on the streets to celebrate the Millennium or for the Royal Wedding for example. Of course even in situations like these there's usually some potential for things to get out of control. But on the other side, militancy without numbers is also clearly a losing game—ending up as isolated, easily repressed and with no connection to anyone else. The numbers on a demonstration and the militancy of the demonstrators can kind of compensate for one another. In Prague the militancy of the demonstrators made up for their relatively small number. In Seattle the reverse was the case—large numbers compensating for relatively little militancy.

Being, in essence a political protest movement, the anti-globalisation movement has a limited constituency and it is not so easy to expand numerically on that basis. There seems no especially easy or obvious way for the movement to 'go forward' except in terms of increasing militancy. In a way, the shooting of Carlo Guiliani in Genoa, although in the grand scheme of things nothing that remarkable, demonstrates the bottom line to this movement. If this movement progresses in terms of escalating violence alone then we will lose, because they have guns and we don't. This demonstrates that perhaps the movement is reaching the limits of a separate political protest movement with no particular social base.

In terms of developing the sort of generalised social struggle that will allow us to go beyond just being a political movement and to begin to be a real anti-capitalist *social* movement, we may have an advantage in Britain precisely because the left doesn't exist here in the same way that it does in Italy. The whole neo-liberal project has had a head-start in Britain, in that after 20 years of Thatcherism, the left has been destroyed here and the power of the unions broken to an unprecedented degree. Of course, the fortunes of the left in general are tied to the fortunes of the class struggle. The left is weak at the moment because the class struggle as a whole is weak. An upsurge in class struggle may see a corresponding upsurge in the left as the various left parties and unions attempt to ride the new wave. If this is so then they will try and control and to rein in any upsurge in struggle and it may well come to nothing. After all, probably the main reason for the failure of the closest thing we've come to a revolution in modern times, in France in 1968, was that workers failed to break with the unions and the unions were successfully able to contain the revolt. On the face of it, the greater strength of the left may make it seem like more is going on over in Italy, but the potential for some sort of revolutionary activity could be greater here, because if there is any sort of upsurge in struggle here, it could stand a greater chance of escaping the control of the left. The whole Thatcherite project was a gamble in a way—they were betting that they could dismantle the whole post-war social-democratic consensus, increasing insecurity, cutting wages and increasing work, without provoking the sort of class struggle that necessitated the introduction of the whole apparatus of the post-war state in the first place. This gamble could go wrong and the whole thing could blow up in their faces. Britain is perhaps in a better situation for this to occur than Italy, and it is precisely this sort of social crisis that could provide some sort of basis for the 'anti-capitalist' movement, allowing it to avoid ending trapped in an escalating cycle of increasing militancy.

You can contact the author of this piece via: SDEF! c/o Prior House, 6 Tilbury Place, Brighton BN2 2GY, UK

> > S E V E N

love changes everything

by V E N U S K A M U R A

My name is Venus Kamura. I am not part of any organisation or religion, but just for now I am a citizen of Planet Earth and part of the human race. The following are just my feelings written after the battle of Gothenburg and the battle of Genoa in the summer of 2001. I want to share them with as many people as possible to try to stop the flow of blood in such a special movement that is global and ancient and in need of change if we are all to bring about the abolition of dict-atorship on this wonderful planet. I want to live in a land where freedom and our hearts will be our leaders and we will all be happy again. I know in my heart that this is possible. Planet Earth is a land of infinite possibilities. Let's get it rockin!

The passion of our commitment to seeing in a new world where we are all One and the planet is saved from the disastrous effects of a "travelling circus of capital-ists" who threaten the destiny of the planet and our children with extinction for the sake of temporary benefits, unsustainable lifestyles, dictatorship and financial reward is coming to a head World-Wide.

Let us not kid ourselves that this is a new movement. This is a movement that has been happening all over the world since the rise of greed and violence. The only difference is that it is our turn in history to do our best for the future of the planet. We must consider carefully our next step, acknowledging history and breaking free from the circle of war and so that we may move harmoniously into the cosmic infinite spiral of change into a beautiful new world. We must move together in harmony expressing the needs of Those we choose to represent and not our own personal feelings of revenge on the police slaves who know not who they are, or, what they are doing by giving their lives up to be just pawns in a dictator's games.

Our recklessness, and acting from our egos could cost lives; it may not even be our own life that we put in jeopardy but the lives of our fellow activists, friends and families, or those we are representing in the most vulnerable countries. We saw in Italy how the state took revenge on our movement as soon as all the G8 guests had left by massacring our sleeping friends in school Diaz that night, not to mention the massacre on the streets during the demonstration.

It is not a personal battle we are here for. It is a vision of hope we carry for everyone. Proceed with caution. Use Your deepest intuition. Be careful not to confuse intuition and fear. Use Your integrity. Use Your heart with the deepest Love for all that is, and all that can be, and we will each be in ourselves the people we want to see in the world we are working together to reinvent. We can and we will live in harmony. There will be peace on Mother Earth and we will all be empowered. There will be no slaves and each person and living thing will feel joy in every day.

That day is coming if we proceed with commitment to global change. If we proceed with the interests of everyone and every living thing on the planet that is being affected by the dictatorship of globalisation, and if we use our macrocosmic view of the world and not the microcosmic short-term view of what we want, we will succeed. This may take time and we must be prepared to commit to that. Seeking fast results can cost lives and can end up recreating the age-old war story that for centuries these lords of death, fear, suffering and disease have been manipulating in order to distract us from what is truly happening in the world. We can win. We can even create a win, win situation where these guys can let go of the crap they come out with and work together with us to create a very much better world. The dictators and bullies are feeling threatened, very threatened. They are on the run and all the time they are looking for places out of the way to have their meetings, only highlighting the need for more global action.

One of the big killers on this planet is apathy. I read a thing in an internet cafe calendar in Galway, Ireland, yesterday that read "why are the people who have all the answers to world problems taxi drivers and hair dressers?" This was a very good skit on human behaviour in general where people have all the answers and yet sit on their asses and don't act on their ideas. Why not? We can and we must empower each other and ourselves and rise above apathy. We need action and we need it now.

If things continue as they are going, scientists tell us, there will be no future of the human race. Some might say that might be a good thing, but everyone and the planet dying is a boring ending and I want a party, a massive global party full of happy loving rocking tick tockin fun and funky free people living in peace, laughing singing dancing and playing like they've never played before. I am counting on being there. We can make a difference. We can change the world.

This day is nearer than we think, so long as we kick ass and create it. This may mean the word Apathy becomes extinct. Why not? Why settle for less than the full change. We can and we will. Come on, it's going to be great. And it's going to be a rocking party to celebrate a rocking victory for the future of the planet. It will be a free party , not like the free party that we have to pay into as seems to happen with the people who are squatting warehouses and aggressively capitalising on the free party scene.We will all have made it through and everybody's names on the guest list. It's going to be the party of a lifetime, all good vibes and it's never going to end.

First things first, we have to outwit these so-called war experts who are set up by the government to set us up. As we saw in Genoa they are trying to get us to run into traps and together with the vulture culture media create a drama to their advantage. They do the same throughout the world. They did it with the Japanese in order to justify in some way dropping the bombs on them and as they have done in the Gulf War and throughout the arab and islamic nations. Globalism has been the main killer of so many people around the world mostly backed by America and the first world nations and due to a special agreement Britain has too much blood on its hands to speak of. Greed and Ignorance has cost too many lives and it's time for it to stop. We must be careful that we as a movement stick together. They will try to divide us. We are all working towards the same thing. We may all have different ways of getting to that point. Police and government are always infiltrating our movement because it threatens their position of power over us. They have set themselves up as leaders of the world and really they only represent their fatcat friends. We must not be divided as a people. We must recognise the tricks they use to turn us against each other. One person who told me they were with the black block when they started smashing up a bank was surprised to have one of the black bloc tell him that it was OK to smash up the bank even though the police were there watching. It was a strange air of confidence that he said that the cops were not going to do anything. That sat strange with my friend. This to me even sounded a bit weird until of course You remember that we are being infiltrated and set up by the police the whole time. It was of course recorded on video police dressed up as demonstrators getting out of police vans and smashing up banks and then going back to their police vans and looking at maps deciding where to go to next. This is not a new trick but it works for them.

Such propaganda is easy whilst we have an easy to hijack group such as those brave and direct action members who we must remember are there for the same reason as us to demonstrate against the recognised leaders of the world, and to have a free world for all. The police target them and hijack them with their dirty tactics, setting them up.

Let's face it, what has destroying a bank got to do with violence. The violence caused through banks corrupt use of money has cost the lives of millions of vulnerable people, and especially those in the most vulnerable countries, not to mention the investments in arms and other non planet and people friendly businesses they invest in. How strange that these banks are so highly regarded while those who highlight it by getting rid of a few are made out to criminals. But Black block are being made out to be criminals by even us. That sucks. This kind of direct action by black block, which, like our ideas and ways of expressing ourselves must not be judged by those of us who express ourselves differently at demonstrations. We must not be divided by our difference of opinion or we will end up being like the political parties who fight for world domination. We all are on the streets for the same reason. We must respect our differences and work out a way of working together. After all we all want a better world and not to recreate a hierarchy of good demonstrators and bad demonstrators. We want One world. One love. Not another stupid fight, fighting among ourselves.

Don't be led into their trap to have us turn against each other. We are one for one.

They are trying to divide us and we must remember even more so to stick together. Some friends of mine were going with the black block at Genoa. At one point they were trying to find another group to run with when they were aggressively attacked and screamed at by other demonstrators. These demonstrators who attacked them were calling themselves pacifists and were attacking them because they walked through the Pacifists Square. Our group had also been in the Pacifists Square previously; the only difference was we wore pink so we didn't get any grief from these so called pacifists.

Then that same group tried to join our group; the pinks and the general consensus seemed to be that we didn't want them. I was really angry at this point of divide, and I said how we were doing the same kind of alienation that our governments do to asylum seekers who try to enter our countries. I was disgusted by the response to not letting in our fellow humans looking for safety, the day after a march on immigration. Such hypocrisy. These people for whatever reason wanted to be with us and were in need of our protection and we were in a serious time of crisis. In such times, it must be obvious that our different political groups mean nothing. It is the lives of our fellow demonstrators and our own lives that must be protected. If we can give support to each other regardless of our politics then we must give it. We must support each other, whatever our colour. If You or I were being beaten up by police there is no doubt in my mind that black block would not hesitate to help us by defending us from the police. We must look at what has happened in war history where governments have turned people against their own people.

They will continue with their dirty tactics, that's how they run the world, but we can and we will work out a way of being direct and effective. Direct action rocks and is important. They use the dirty way. We don't need to. The whole world is watching our movement and if we proceed with our truth and don't fall into their traps we win quicker. They are relying on us being violent and aggressive so that they can show the general public the need to criminalise our strength and our threat to them. They want to make us out to be terrorists to give them the go ahead to squash our global and strong movement. This is the same propaganda they use to start wars, they frighten people into believing we are evil terrorists. Be careful: our actions could put the whole movement in danger not just for ourselves but for the people around the world we are choosing to represent. Cop bashing, however much of a buzz at the time and a great point scorer, doesn't save the world and is a distraction. It is also the distraction the real terrorists, the government want from us. Growing up in Ireland I have seen them do the same thing with groups there. We all know how the kids on the streets suddenly became not political prisoners but imprisoned criminal terrorists due to a quick law and were allowed to rot in prison on hunger strike even Bobby Sands a member of Margaret Thatcher's Parliment. These cops, or boys with toys and no brains can be dangerous, but they are thickos, and are a waste of time. They are a decoy from the guys who are the real enemy. We need to go straight to the beast and get them to fight their own battle. I would love to see a battle of truths with all the citizens of the world as a jury. Finding an honest judge would be a treat too. Well, why not put them on trial for all the crimes towards Mother Earth and her children.

Each of us in this world has a very important power, we can all love. LOVE CHANGES EVERYTHING. We all, each one of us, have this love tool inside of us always waiting to be activated. Love is the greatest power of all. It can change more situations than any other. We can all proceed with this energy, putting it everywhere we go into everyone we meet and everything we do.

Consumer choice is a huge part of that. We respect each other, our planet and ourselves by shopping against the grain of capitalism. We boycott everything possible to do with abuse of our people and our planet and we boycott also the large supermarkets who profit from these businesses. Demonstrations are good and important but just as important is boycotting. Boycotting is effective and beautiful easy and is also something anyone can do. As with recycling and planting trees and spreading a good vibe rather than a bad one. It can take a bit of getting used to for some but the rewards are huge as we stop living off the backs of the future generations and create a deeper sense of the planet's needs. Don't forget household cleaners are environmentally sick and deadly. There is so much we can do and it's good fun too. We can make the world the place we want it to be and we have a chance to save the rivers and the seas for swimming in for the children of tomorrow.

I really fear our anti-capitalist movement could, by taking things personally, take a wrong turn and end up with an elite movement of hardened anarchists who are only there to take on the police. It is at this point that they win again. They will have forced us into their war. Well, we don't play war games. We want a fair world so we don't play dirty. It's really boring playing dirty. It has happened for too long. Let's just stick to our integrity and be really aware of the people and planet we are representing and stick to our super hero tactics. Without violence we are the Bat Woman, Bat Man, Spider Woman or Spider Man, Super Woman or Super Man, or Scooby Doo kids who always get the bad guys and turn from being seen as the pesky meddling kids into the saviours of the universe. Yeah, come on kids. Please let's do it this way. It's Love that rocks every living thing. So let's do it with Love. Here's To Peace On Earth Now...

lots of Love

Venus x

If You would like to read more or add your opinion please contact Venusrockingtheworld@yahoo.com ... since this was written George Bush has found an excuse to attack those who they have been attacking for as long as I can ever remember and has set themselves up with the same old tactics. Tony Blair who wants to be George Bush offers the support. It is not known who made the inevitable attack on America but it is sure who will suffer. They now as with the Japanese bombing are receiving support from the people. In the same week that the arms fair takes place in London, and as I said on my banner there "Fighting For Peace is Like Fucking For Virginity". Let Peace and Love remain in all our hearts and may this be resolved without bloodshed.

> > E I G H T

strange times

by SIOBHAN

We travelled to Genoa by flying to a different city as we were completely paranoid that we wouldn't get in, and by outrageous good luck got chatting to an Italian kid who gave us a lift in his car all the way to the centre of Genoa, stopping off to have tea at his house with his parents! They said they supported the demonstration but didn't like violence and we talked about that for a while, they were really nice people. The young guy worked at McDonalds as it was the only job in his town and to help us get into the city we put McDonalds paraphernalia all over the inside of the car. I don't think it made much difference really, probably the more important thing was the local number plates.

Arriving at Genoa was the most surreal experience, it was a lovely evening and we were walking across this beautiful Mediterranean port town at sunset which appeared to contain all the police in the world. They were putting up the steel walls which were to keep us out of the conference and we had to walk through all these groups of carabinieri, soldiers and a bewildering range of other types of police, including secret police, we went to a cafe and had to leave as it was full of secret police. It was hard to walk through the big groups of armed carabinieri feeling like you had a neon sign above your head saying rentamob. The police strength was so overwhelming I suggested we just went home straightaway. We got to the convergence point without problems and met friends. The next day we had to start making plans, we realised we had been so convinced we would not get in, that we had no idea what to do. We went to the second half of one meeting of the pink block but we never got it together to go to any other meetings, which we regretted later. We went to the Carlini stadium which had a real buzz about it, full to the brim of people making banners and

props including some brilliant papier mache pigs with the flags of all the G8 countries for the tongues. There I made probably my most constructive contribution to the whole event by washing up the cooking pots. That night there was a brilliant concert by Manu Chao, the only time I've been in a concert where instead of waving their lighters in the air people waved their crash helmets. If we had tried to storm the Red Zone right then I think we would have got through by sheer adrenalin.

On Thursday we went on the migrants demonstration which had I think 60,000 people. The number of migrants really was pretty low but it was good to see banners in Turkish and Arabic and my favourite, in Italian, said "No boss, no border." The energy of so many people in the narrow streets with drums and music was really something and on this demo I felt probably the most positive of all the weekend. We marched with a group from southern Spain and there was a real effort made at singing in different languages, in Italian, in Spanish, in English, both serious chants like 'No borders, no nations' or 'No person is illegal' and silly ones like 'We want bread, we want wine, we want Berlusconi hanging from a pine'. I was annoyed by the number of national flags, such as Basque or Cuban, on a supposedly anti-nation state demo, but that was the way it was for the weekend with many issues.

Then Red Zone Day dawned and still we had not made any plan so we just split into different demonstrations, some with the Tute Bianche, some with the Black Block, one with a trade union section and it was decided that I was to stay in the Carlini stadium as I am slightly disabled and it was thought by my friends to be too dangerous. In the campsite people were making homemade armour and we saw one very well disciplined demo goer doing press-ups outside his tent at daybreak. As everyone marched out together we looked like some kind of post apocalyptic punky army, straight out of *Judge Dredd*, and someone shouted out "Remember folks, blend in and act normal!" As I walked up to Carlini there was the bizarre sight of a beautiful panoramic view of Genoa with three police helicopters moving in circles in the sky like mosquitoes in an otherwise still landscape. At Carlini the demonstration was leaving very late and so I watched all the different groups moving out, a lot of people very padded out to twice their normal body mass with plastic shields, crash helmets and some with huge papier mache carrots—don't ask me why. It was a moment of great excitement with people singing "The people united will never be defeated" in French, in Greek, in Italian, although I was very aware that some people had already been on the streets for an hour or more and I don't know why the demonstration left late. Eventually everyone was gone and I settled down to wait.

Some hours later I was standing outside the Carlini stadium watching the crowds coming back, when a friend told me, "They killed someone." I asked some Italian people if they knew where the murdered person was from, and they said 'Espagnol'. My partner is Spanish and I tried not to panic but it was impossible, the Italian bloke gave me some whisky and took me to the information point, where he told them the situation and said we needed to know the name. They didn't have it and I ended up in a room with a computer hooked up to the internet with a picture, where I was supposed to look at this picture of the murdered body and identify if it was my boyfriend.

I couldn't, partly because of the nature of the picture which I'm sure you would recognise, where Carlo is lying face down in his own blood and wearing a mask. Partly there was a huge crowd of people around the computer, some of them I think might have been with him earlier and had to identify who it was in the picture, I just understood that they were saying "E lui" (it's him) over and over again. And the third reason is that I couldn't handle the situation, as obviously I did not want to recognise him. I gave up and a woman understood my situation and gave me a description, she said "...and he had a tattoo on his back" and I knew it was not my partner, she hugged me and I cried and cried as the relief I felt made me feel so guilty as, OK it was not my boyfriend lying dead in the road but it was bound to be the friend and the son and the brother of somebody, and I realised that tonight so many people would be going through this process of finding out if it was their friend or not and for some of them it would have a happy ending like me but not for everybody.

When I got back to the campsite that night, as I approached the gate there was a stream of people leaving with their tents on their backs. One German woman, in tears, said that the camp had been disowned by GSF and was now illegal, that this meant the police could come any time and raid the camp as we had no legal protection. I don't know if this was true, some people the next day said otherwise, that the GSF definitely had not denounced any camp. I only can say that a lot of people certainly thought it was true, and that apparently the police did attack the camp with tear gas after we left and arrested anyone who tried to enter, but they did this to all our spaces at one time or another, it doesn't prove anything either way. At the time I didn't know anything, I was only afraid that I might never find my friends if we had to leave. I went to my camp and to my extreme relief my friends all returned that night, stinking to high heaven of tear gas it's true, but they all returned.

The next morning we went to the convergence point and this was the beginning of what was in some ways the worst thing of the whole event for me, because there I discovered how much bad feeling there was inside the demonstration, a lot of blame in particular was being directed at the Black Block for the death of Carlo Guiliani and for the violence of the police. Some comrades of mine were abused by a group of people shouting that "It was your fault Carlo Guiliani was killed, it was your fault we were beaten by the police." This debate continued for weeks in fact even after we returned home and I felt in a very contradictory position. It was especially difficult as I had not been there and so I could not have any real informed perspective, and had to hear wildly different accounts without any basis to judge them. I felt strongly that dangerous or not I wanted to go on the demonstration because it was important to me now that someone had been killed to go and be one more on the streets even if I was useless in any practical way. I found a compromise that I would go but avoid danger. I was often in a difficult position because of the physical danger posed by the police tactics which meant that I felt marginalised and useless, I don't know how we could have dealt with this problem.

The demonstration was huge, 300,000 I was told. As we were walking back we saw an incredible sight, literally incredible as in that I thought I was hallucinating, of a line of blue tanks with POLIZIA painted on them, driving down the street, so many that it looked like the Mayday parade in Moscow, I was looking around for Brezhnev on a balcony somewhere. It was much like a victory parade in fact, that they were flaunting their strength and demonstrating their power to control the streets. In this

The body of Carlo Giuliani, murdered by the forces of the Italian state

atmosphere of defeat we went to the Brignole station and here too the police were attempting to assert their dominance by continually coming in and in some instances taunting the crowd, any time they showed their faces there was a strong response from the people shouting "Assassini! Assassini!" with so many voices in unison inside the station it did make the hairs on the back of your neck stand up and could have made a difference in making them think twice about trying to pull anybody out of the crowd. There was one incident when they did try to arrest someone, which happened when a man came to announce that the police were attacking the Indymedia centre. People started to put on their rucksacks to go down there but then nobody seemed to actually go, maybe some went from other platforms. It could be that everyone was prepared to if other people went but no-one was exactly gagging for a fight, this represented for me the depth of our defeat that we were not prepared collectively to go and defend our comrades because we felt we had been comprehensively beaten and we didn't want any more. When the next day we saw the horrific images of the attack on the school with pools of blood on the floor and splashed on the walls we were sickened that we had been a couple of thousand people in the train station and had done nothing to prevent it. We waited maybe six hours for our train but in an atmosphere with a lot of camaraderie, as every train left people sang and raised their fists out of the windows and everybody shared water and cigarettes. When the train finally arrived it seemed that all our problems were over, of course they weren't as we were yet to find out about the school and to spend three days frantically looking for information about our friends. But when that train arrived and we knew we were definitely going to leave Genoa alive it seemed the only important thing in the world.

an italian job

by B E C K Y

US VERSUS 18,000 POLICE

Like many or even most people travelling to Genoa from abroad, this wasn't to be my first experience of a mass demo with masses of police. I was sure I had never been anywhere with 18,000 cops but couldn't quite visualise what that meant. In fact, nothing could really have prepared me for what was in store for us in Genoa. What we experienced was an all-out police state.

Cops everywhere, guns everywhere, tanks for god's sake! The whole city was tear gassed. Tear gas was thrown from helicopters and 8th floor apartments. Only luck saved you from severe beatings and charges. Not even pacifists and official looking people, like lawyers were safer. I even heard a group of nuns got a beating and this is catholic Italy we're talking about. Basically they just wanted to beat shit out of everyone they got their hands on to and if you intervened, like a friend of mine, you found yourself with the barrel of a gun down your throat, as well as getting the shit kicked out of you of course. People were ferried to their sleeping place by special buses. 'Don't go out on the streets alone' came the announcement late on Friday after the murder of Carlo Giuliani to all packed into the convergence centre at Piazzale Kennedy. Helicopters circled over specifically to provoke, drowning out half of what people were saying. 'In fact, don't go out in small groups, or large groups, in fact don't go out at all, it isn't safe, wait for the buses'. Yes, police state is the only way of describing things.

The city centre was behind a 5 metre fence. The rest of the city was completely emptied out. Practically every shop boarded up with notices, 'Closed for G8'. There was no doubt as to the extent to which the State was prepared to go. The Red Zone

was unbelievable. I arrived on the evening they were erecting the barriers. Five metres of metal mesh blocking off every side road leading into the city centre. The work was carried out systematically in almost complete silence. The barriers were high but not particularly strong and impenetrable.

We zigzagged in and out of the Red Zone until the final central pieces of the barrier were slotted into place and we were on the outside. Of course we could join the call to break down the Red Zone, but not until the small matter of 18,000 cops had been dealt with.

We already knew before we arrived that 200 body bags had been made available by Genoa city council. It was a bit of a joke among those of us preparing to go to Genoa. Talk about unfunny jokes.

So what happened? Why was this such a different experience than anything we'd ever done before?

First of all it wasn't really so different. There had been massive repression of all major demos for the past couple of years. Just a few months before in Naples the police violence had been terrifying and people had complained of torture and seriously hard beatings in police cells. In Gothenburg three people were shot, one almost killed. Genoa was worse but no so different. In fact we expected it, we just weren't prepared for it.

Repression on demos had got steadily worse in Italy over the past few years after a good decade of fairly low key protest. Things started to change around the time that the more mainstream protest movement adopted confrontational and unusual tactics during demos. In a similar way to RTS (J18, for example changed the climate of repression in this country), in Italy Tute Bianche actions over the past few years have led to more repression. Gone are the old days of compromise with the police over demos and negotiations on the level and content of protest. I mean, there are just some things you can't tell the cops beforehand that you're going to do, and when you take them by surprise they get pretty pissed off. It's not about things getting out of hand and fighting with the police. That was and is always going to happen. It's about changing the goal posts that have been there for a number of years or taking them away completely.

The participation of Italian groups in anti-globalisation protests over the past couple of years and the internationalisation of protest have contributed to this change. The dominance of the non-institutionalised left, direct action groups, centri sociali, pacifist associations as well as the adoption of radical tactics during the demos have marked a new era. For example, the still massively influential Rifondazione Comunista found itself overshadowed by the Tute Bianche and Agnoletto (leader of GSF) both before and during the anti-G8 protests in Genoa.

The State have no qualms about bashing liberals and pacifists but tend to draw the line when it comes to other power sharers. The only square on Friday that appeared to be left well alone with no police presence, was the Rifondazione Comunista one. Although many of the rank and file members of Rifondazione were elsewhere and getting a good beating, their MPs were safe and sound. Then again, if all Rifondazione want to do is win elections it's not surprising they left the Red Zone intact.

One of the most common comments during Genoa was that it was all Berlusconi's fault. Of course we all hate Berlusconi, (Best chant: Mano Negra clandestino, Berlusconi ASSASSINO, Berlusconi ASSASSINO Berlusconi ILLEGAL) and his team of fascists but I think that the international forces of law and order had been planning this one long before Berlusconi's election victory. And of course the same level of repression would have been on the cards, had the previous centre left government still been in power. They were there during the Naples protests, which although small, were ferocious and contributed to the rising wave of repression. (It is amazing to think that the centre left coalition had the cheek to threaten to join the march on the 21st when they had organised the bloody summit when they were in power just a few months before).

However, the Berlusconi dynamic isn't to be completely discounted.

There was to be no pretence of the right to democratic protest. He and his cabinet of fascists were not going to be too upset if their police force got a bit too heavy-handed, that was for sure. Coupled with this was the problem of the police themselves. Fascist culture in the police has remained unchallenged since the end of the Resistance. The brand of old-style Fascism where everyone is a communist and communists deserve a good beating whatever. They no doubt would have been encouraged by Gianfranco Fini's[*] harsh words and would feel protected by the heavy presence of fascists in Government. If they needed any encouragement to exaggerate, they had it.

*Gianfranco Fini, Secretary of fascist Alleanza Nazionale party and Berlusconi's Vice President.

The other dynamic said to have added to the level of police violence and repression is of course property destruction and Black Block tactics. Of course we know that the cops didn't need to attack nuns, throw tear gas into an ambulance, smash computers, attack people while sleeping etc etc. in order to keep the level of peace required by the Home Secretary and the TV watching public. Rioting in Genoa was more of a function for police violence than reason for it and we would all do well to learn the lessons from that, but it is false to think that, had the Black Block not smashed banks the police would not have found another excuse to unleash all that pre-planned violence. I mean, it's not as if they suddenly had to draft in reinforcements, or they were taken by surprise. It was all there, ready and waiting for us regardless of what we did. It's also not as if the police were subtle in their tactics in the hope that people would think they were only attacking when attacked by black block or to protect property. The Scuola Diaz attack shows that the police didn't need an excuse to make what they did appear reasonable. The systematic violent repression of anti-G8 protesters, whatever their tactics or politics, was decided and organised well before the black block smashed in their first bank. The attack was orchestrated after J18, after Seattle, after Prague, after Gothenburg by international intelligence and joint police committees of all G8 nations. The lack of widespread condemnation after the shootings in Gothenburg gave the go-ahead to fill at least one of those 200 body bags.

However, that is not to say that the police didn't appear to have used black block elements of the protest in their general tactics, not as an excuse to beat people but in an attempt to discredit and split the movement and play off some parts of the protest against the others.

The police tried to portray everyone as baddies and tried to manipulate the Black Block in order to do that. They tried and in part they succeeded and in part failed.

The failure came from the fact that, first of all, their attempts were laughingly unsubtle and even the worst right wing commentators were forced to admit that actually the real baddies were the cops themselves. Images of bank trashing and the array of 'weapons' gathered, black T-shirts with skulls, Swiss army knives and crash helmets paled into insignificance in the face of police beating the shit out of protesters and the attack on the Scuola Diaz. The exception to this was the murder of Carlo Giuliani which had more complex reactions and which the police have been more successfully able to manipulate to their own gain.

Secondly, difficult to dispute or explain evidence of police infiltration and manipulation of Black Block has emerged. There is that photo of a 'black block affinity group', posing outside the police station along with other uniformed police. There's the footage of those two 'black block types' getting out of a Carabinieri van and disappearing into the crowd, just got away with a caution? I don't think so.

This kind of police tactic rings home loud and hard in a country where less than 30 years ago the State was responsible for bombing and killing tens of innocent people in an attempt to raise the tension of political conflict and justify massive repression and reduction in civil liberties.

The manipulation of the black block issue also had a massive effect on people

witnessing its effects in Genoa. A group of young pacifist women were in no doubt as to what happened when some Black Block ran into their demo in Piazza Manin on Friday in an attempt to mix in and become invisible after being chased by the police. They were politely told to fuck off and after they made themselves scarce, the police began the first of four massive charges on the pacifists, hospitalising the two friends of the woman who told me this. This has a lasting effect on people who, for the first time, see the forces of law and order stripped down to their bare core and see what they are really there for. In fact, it appeared to me that people who became radicalised by what they saw in Genoa were far less prepared to spend time laying into the Black Block for their smash and run techniques than those of us who didn't need Genoa to understand the real role of the police as protectors of capital not people and the lengths they are prepared to go to do this.

Yes, it was the more radical elements of the Italian protest. Tute Bianche and other Centri Sociali who appeared to have found their number 1 enemy in the Black Block. And that brings us to US. Us being the protesters as a whole.

US

The first thing to say about the organisation of the protest as a whole is that it was an Italian affair and it incorporated just about everyone from the Italian left. There were not only those who had been involved in other anti-globalisation protests like Tute Bianche, Rete Lilliput and Rifondazione Comunista but also those who hadn't—Cobas, FIOM (Metalworkers Union), other Centri Sociali. This was a huge event and everyone was there. In terms of numbers, this was a bit of a first for the anti-global movement. Others had been small or in countries where the left was not so big and influential as in Italy. Those who went to Prague were uncomfortable about the lack of Czech involvement. Meetings were conducted in English and the organisation was dominated by foreigners. Let's say Genoa was about as far away from that as you can imagine.

This brings with it all the problems of travelling to a demo in another country. You don't speak the language, you don't know the political groupings. You don't know how to identify people politically and vice versa ("There's a train load of anarchists arriving from Britain called something like 'resist globalisation'"). You don't know the usual procedures of organisation and someone else's organisational fuck-up can quickly become your organisational fuck-up. All this is confusing and potentially a bit of a nightmare. The best way around all this, of course, was to create alliances beforehand, which is fine except that for many anarchists and people who wanted to do black block, the reference point was Italian anarchists who were already outside the organisation of the demo. In the months leading up to Genoa, there had been conflict between Tute Bianche and some sections of the Italian Anarchist movement about hegemony of protest tactics. The result of the conflict was the breakdown in communication and the identification of the other as: Tute Bianche, another institutional group at best and at worst 'police in white', and the Anarchist groups as nihilist and dangerous individualists... This created a logistical problem for the black block for the 20th.

On the 20th Genoa was split into what were called 'thematic squares', that is, each group had their own space and did their own thing—all to the general objective of breaking down the Red Zone or throwing balloons over the Red Zone or marching to the Red Zone etc etc. The main problem that emerged was that there was no space for the Black Block. This was not because there was some secret meeting place but because there was no meeting place at all.

This logistical problem was compounded by the fact that those wanting to do Black Block things, of course, saw the 20th, Direct Action day, as 'their day'. The 19th was the immigrants march which would be non-violent. People were happy to stick to that knowing that the next day was the designated day for a riot. And Saturday was the unions and Communist Party march—maybe a good day to go to the beach. Of course, as we know, all that changed.

What emerged from the day was that actually no-one actually managed to do anything they had planned. The Black Block, although successful in property destruction, didn't really find the best place to do it and ended up pissing off many of the other protesters by invading their spaces. Cobas didn't march after clashes with Black Block and police. The Tute Bianche didn't even leave their stadium until 4pm. The pacifist march was crushed and dispersed by the police. This, along with the murder of Carlo Giuliani and hundreds of injuries, with hundreds of others fearing for their lives was the result of the direct action day. After months of preparation the whole thing was a disaster. It has to be said that Black Block stole the show and the organisers of the demo were never going to be happy about that. This, along with objective mistakes made by Black Block, paved the way for them to become the scapegoat for all those who felt the need.

In a way, the media have won their battle, imposing a representation of the protest in terms of colours, uniforms and factions. The fact that the Tute Bianche played the media game didn't help much. The mutation of our tactics is the only tool we have to avoid this trap, the trap of being the actors in a plot we did not write. In the theatre of Genoa, tactics are the only identifying elements of groups while the different voices were not heard. Certainly, the real voices of people in the Black Block weren't heard. They were the "useless rioters". Most of the comrades who express their ferocious criticism of the Black Block had no idea what Black Block actually meant, or the complex political make-up of individuals who choose property destruction as a form of political protest. Their criticism is formed only on the basis of the Black Block 'tactic'.

The Tute Bianche confused the simulation of struggle with the struggle itself and found themselves lost when the State decided not to play their game. What was new and innovative at first place became ritual and therefore self-indulgent. Some actors weren't even mentioned as they didn't have a media-friendly identity, i.e. FIOM and even the Cobas.

While we continue to identify ourselves and others by tactics rather than aims or ideas, we run the risk of sticking so rigidly to those tactics as to make them the most important thing in our struggle. Our struggle is not a struggle for identity and the defending of roles and tactics at all costs makes sense only within and not beyond our movement.

Once a protest movement weaves its way into the whole fabric of society, starts to make complete sense to people and connects with their everyday lives and personal struggles against capitalism, protest tactics and group identities will find their rightful place as tools to arrive at our main political objectives.

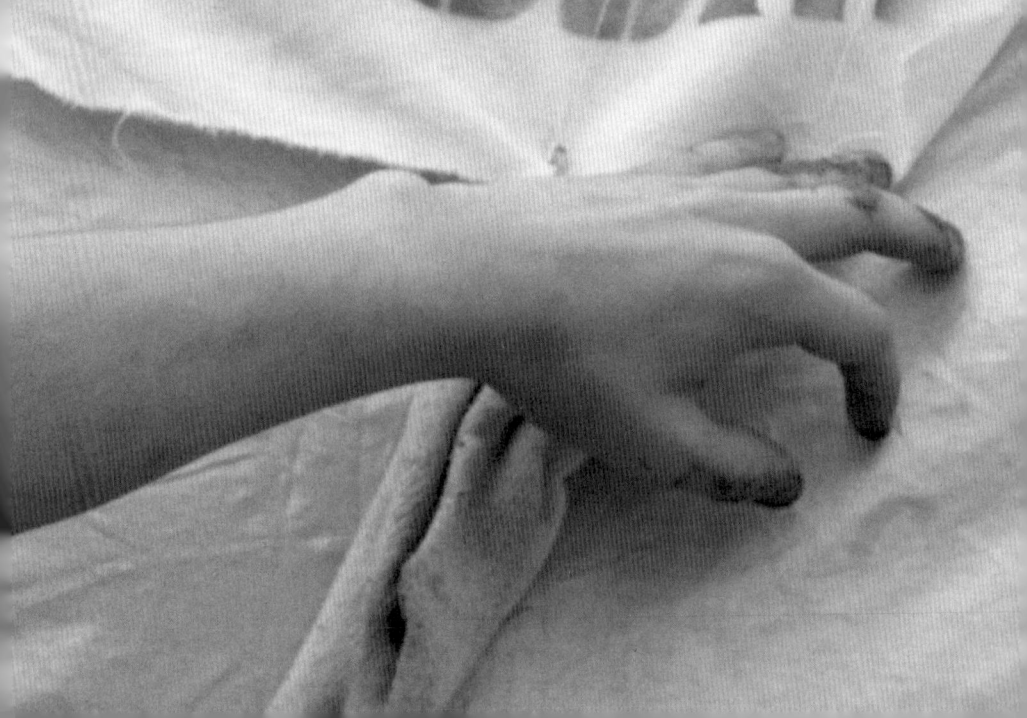

it was like this before...

by A D A M P O R T E R

So what really happened in Genoa? Were there riots? Sure. Was there destruction? Sure. Did the police go mad? You bet. With authority from on high. And we don't mean the Pope.

The first march, made up of around 40,000 people, went off peacefully on Thursday. Police were persuaded to back off and put down their guns. All the various groups marched. There was no trouble and, of course, no coverage in the media.

Friday was different. We arrived in town as the so-called Black Block were cutting a swathe through the city. They had been burning cars. They had been attacking shops, most of which represented some form of power, mainly banks. But they also attacked and burned the cars of very ordinary people. Fiat 126s lay upside down, unlikely ever to have been in the hands of an oppressor. There were also pet shops, grocery stores and smaller outlets whose repressive power was negligible. It wasn't a great sight.

Firstly, the block were out on their own. They weren't heading for the fence around the summit and they weren't even heading for the police. Their attacks lacked symbolism. The average age of the attendees, mainly Italian and German, was very young. They seem to have accepted a view of 'anarchy' that, amazingly, is the one put forward by the people they claim to hate, people like Tony Blair and Silvio Berlusconi. Both this 'block' that we saw and the leaders we despise so much seem to hold the view that anarchy is based on chaos and destruction rather than a well thought-out political ideology defined by compassion and self-governance.

The block was unopposed by the police. The police had allowed them to set up barricades, burn and loot. Why? It is difficult to fathom because when the peaceful marchers turned up, the police reaction was very different. Almost certainly the free-dom given to chunks of the Black Block was designed as an 'excuse' to attack the peaceful demonstrations. Arguments raged afterwards about the level of 'infiltration'. Some people, who mainly weren't there, said the Black Block were filled full of under-cover policemen. It's rubbish. There were infiltrators, they were photographed, but they infiltrated to watch and photograph, not to lead the group.

As a movement we must not fall into traps laid by the authorities. Some of these traps remind me of the sort of nonsense trotted out about football hooligans. The 'Black Block' are not some sort of centralised army, they can be joined by anyone wearing black. Whether 'ideological' Black Blockers object or not, it's the truth, espe-cially on the ground. So these acts are far more spontaneous than some sort of wild conspiracy painted by the media. We would do well not to repeat their claims.

Also the 'harm' that the Block did was nothing to what the police did. What I think a lot of other demonstrators, including those who fought back against the police, would say is why were the Block not taking on the police? Why were they not taking on the fence? When it all kicked off... where were they? But they are a part of the movement, a valuable part, a young part and their energy and determination should not be wasted, just better directed.

So, as the so-called Tute Bianche, the White Overalls, marched down the road around 20,000 strong, they got stuck in a side road. They were preparing to come out into the main road towards the police-designated Red Zone, the area contained behind the 20-foot-high, steel-mesh fences. The Tute Bianche, by the way, is a direct action group that is opposed to violence. They pad and mask themselves to avoid attack by the police. But as they prepared to turn the corner, police opened fire with rounds of tear gas. Everyone, including ourselves, was overcome by the gas. Forced to flee, blind and choking with thousands of others. It was a wonder no-one died there and then.

But then the police got their reaction. The crowds fought them back. However, unlike the Black Block, this was reactive rather than pre-meditated. Vans and lines of carabinieri, the paramilitary police, came under attack from stones, sticks and anything else to hand. Fighting was fierce. Police drove their armoured vans through the crowds, the majority of whom were still escaping, at 40 or 50 miles an hour. How no-one died there and then is still beyond us. And of course all the time there was tear gas. Round after round of tear gas.

After a period of being gassed, you became immune. The panic dropped. The eight-inch-long canisters were pumped through the air with such regularity that you could watch them coming and run accordingly. They made a high-pitched whirring sound, and when they hit the floor they fizzed thick white clouds. Burning like power burned in the nostrils of the 'leaders' encamped on their luxury cruise liner just a couple of miles away.

No-one was immune. Journalists, locals, men and women were all subject to fierce beatings from the police. One woman we found, her head dripping rapidly congealing blood, had been attacked by seven officers. Obviously very hard men. The fact that she was a journalist had made no difference. Italian TV too showed picture after picture of police attacking indiscriminately. A local woman (almost

certainly not even involved in the protests), in every other way a chubby 50-year-old Italian *mama*, was beaten to the ground by four well-armed carabinieri.

Then there was Carlo Giuliani. A police Land Rover was attacked. Not surrounded as some claimed—pictures taken by Dylan Martinez of Reuters confirmed this to be a lie. Nor was Giuliani hit by a rock as the police first claimed. He was shot in the head with live ammunition by a frightened 20-year-old conscript policeman, while his more experienced comrades-in-gas watched from mere yards away. After they shot him, they reversed the Land Rover over him, then gassed him just to be sure. But they got it right first time. He was dead and they had upped the stakes.

So to the Saturday. An enormous peaceful march of 150,000 people. A teeming sea of bodies of all descriptions. The march went along the seafront towards a line of police but then took a right turn. A selection of the organisers went to the police line near the Red Zone. They were almost immediately gassed. The police also fired a canister into the restaurant area reserved for protestors by the seaside.

Around two minutes later, the police opened fire with around 15 canisters, filling the air with smoke. Clouds of it wafted over into nearby residences, loads of it blew back into the faces of the police. For around ten minutes the police, seemingly without any aim or reason, fired canister after canister into the crowd. A crowd that was not even heading towards them. Until then.

People were raising their hands in the air. Asking the police to stop and be restrained like they were on Thursday. But to no avail. Soon protestors were throwing the tear gas back at the police. The gas canisters that were being fired, seemingly indiscriminately, at the restaurant area were taken and thrown into the sea. Soon the

scenario the carabinieri appreared to desire came true. Those most angry with the gassing moved to the front and began to fight back. Litter bins were set alight, the acrid smell of burning plastic mixed with the tingle of the gas. Later the BBC would claim on the World Service that "a group of protestors broke away and attacked the police with rocks". This was pure fantasy. On Saturday the police demanded war and they didn't get it, so they did the next best thing.

They chased thousands of innocent people back down the seafront. Those at the head of the crowd fought them back, the rest at the tail-end made up the peaceful demo. One man told us his story. "We were trying to hold up the old boys. You know, the ones at the back of the protest. But they were trying to hold their wives. No-one could see, they were all choking on the gas. We were shouting at them, 'Go with the crowd, go with the crowd. Keep walking.' Then they (the police) started firing these amazing tear-gas bombs. Like doodlebugs. With fins and wings and stuff. They were 18-inches, two-foot long, but they had no control over them. One ended up in the sea; the others were flying all over the place, right over the heads of the people fighting the police at the front. It was like... what the fuck are they doing?"

After the debacle on the seafront, we walked back down. There were literally hundreds of tear-gas containers littering the street. It stuck to every pore of your body. It surrounded you just like they surrounded the Genoa Social Forum later that night. The Genoa Social Forum, if you missed it, was a building set up by a coalition of various groups to let the independent media get access to the internet and phones. It was the place where the heads of the various groups held press conferences. There was a medical centre and a floor for the indymedia people. On Saturday night, police raided the building saying it was home to the—by now much-mentioned—Black Block. It wasn't.

What the police wanted was revenge for people fighting back on their terms, and they took it. Twelve demonstrators were taken out on stretchers. The walls and floors were coated in blood. Lawyers were attacked. Women were attacked. Some in their sleep. One woman had her wrist broken while she was sleeping. Documents, films and computer equipment were taken away.

We were staying in the Novotel. It was media central. The papers, the TV crews, the radio people, they were all there. To many corporate media journalists, it was the first time they had seen the brutality of the police at first hand. One, who had been near the killing of Giuliani, had been severely beaten by them. He had a stitched head and a broken wrist. He pulled up his T-shirt to show us his official G8 accreditation pass. It was filled with blood, his own. He was too scared for us to photograph him. "Please, please understand me," he said.

We did. Because he had good reason. On the Sunday morning after the raid we woke to find the Novotel surrounded by carabinieri vans. Were they there to protect us? Doubtful since they had not been there on the two previous days during the trouble. Were they there to make sure we left town? Well, we thought we would ask someone who knew.

Because there was a member of the BBC's World Service Spanish division staying at the hotel. He had been around a few years. He said he recognised the patterns. Demonise, attack, demonise, attack. All the time backed up by a faithful right wing/liberal supporting cast of local officials, politicians and the media. "I know this," he said "I know this well, it was like this before, in Chile, under Pinochet."

the tracks of our tears

by J A Z Z

Well, here it is. Genoa—warts and all. This is going to be an honest and straightforward account. There is no point in fantasies or dreams, that's not how we are going to challenge the beast. We need to be open with each in order to develop our tactics.

But first of all, I would like to start at the beginning—why I went to Genoa, because that is too often missed. I went to Genoa because I am against capitalism—let's name the beast: capitalism. I went to Genoa because I believe that capitalism hasn't and can't meet our needs and is a social system that condemns the vast majority of people to stunted and unfulfilled lives despite our best efforts. As that old slogan says, there must be more to life than this. There must be more to life than money, there must be a better way of living than a world where money is more important than human life.

Often people talk of statistics that come from the so-called 'developing' world—those are important because that is at least partly where the wealth of the so-called 'developed' world comes. But it is also a trap to just think of the situation away from this country—what about all the shit that is going down here? Our rulers might think that they are living in the lap of cosy capitalist comfort but for many of us, that simply isn't true. It's not just a matter of not having money to get by, it's a matter of social isolation, the society of anxiety that breeds anxiety: welcome to paedophilia-paranoia land, the land of CCTV, the surveillance society where big brother really is watching you (even though he might be dozing off at the desk because he's on a 12 hour shift and doing another job to keep things together—another contradiction of capitalism).

There was this article recently that had the pay figures for people in this country. In the last two years, top company executives have had pay rises of an average of 29%. According to *Management Today* (sounds great, doesn't it), British chief executives now take home on average an annual salary of £509,000—I reckon that would keep the wolf away from the door. Bosses in this country are better paid than anywhere else in the world apart from (no surprise here) the USA. At the same time manufacturing workers in this country earn the lowest wages in any of the world's developed countries while working longer hours than anywhere else in Europe. And on it goes—and they expect us to be happy bunnies?

Under Tony Blair and the Labour Party, the gap between rich and poor has widened (while under John Major's Conservative government of 1992–97 it actually narrowed). To make it personal, Blair has just authorised his own pay increase by a miserly £47,000 a year. While this has been going on, the number of deaths at work has increased by 34% in the year 2000–2001: 295 workers have been killed at work, six a week on average, another successful statistic for Blair and New Labour. As has been said "Ten Thousand Pharaohs, Five Billion Slaves": kind of sums it all up on one level. On another level is the fact that the state and capitalism are in our own heads—it's the cop in our minds that has helped to keep the pharaohs sitting pretty. That's the score—there's a very small number of people in this world who are experiencing untold wealth that the rest of us can't even dream about, it is so beyond our imagination.

At the same time, these pharaohs, surrounded by their trappings of wealth, defend their power and privileges with utmost ferocity. Ironically, they talk of the 'diminishing' state and some of the liberal commentators such as Noreena Hertz seem to actually believe that the problem is that the state does not have enough power to control those 'nasty' corporations. What in reality has happened over the last 20 years is that the state has shed its social roles (imposed on it by the working class after the Second World War) and increased its repressive roles. One of the first things that Margaret Thatcher did on coming to power in Britain in 1979 was to substantially increase police pay.

The state—whether in the USA, Britain or European Union—has never been more powerful: just take a look at the armoury of the police! The other great weakness with this argument à la Noreena Hertz is that it assumes that the state and the corporations have divergent interests—not so, their interests are primarily one and the same although like any closely knit family they will argue at times over the spoils. The state and the corporations are fundamentally alike.

As an example of state power, in this country—nice, liberal Britain as some people might pretend while reading their *Guardian* and listening to Jeremy Paxman— since 1969 over 1,000 people have died in police custody and yet not one single officer has ever been convicted of any charge relating to these deaths. In the most advanced capitalist country—the USA—over 2,000,000 people in prison, prisons that are run by private companies for profit. We now have the bizarre situation of prison labour in the USA undercutting the wage costs of 'developing' world countries. And we talk of 'developed' and 'developing'...

But whether 'developed' or 'developing', capitalism always needs growth— everything must continue to grow. This effectively means that corporations like General Motors have an ideal world in which every individual owns a car, preferably two—a car, mind you, that is built-in to fail after a relatively short period of time (far shorter than technologically necessary). This drive for more and more growth is at the heart of capitalism which means it is unreformable. All that capitalism can think of is short-term profit and very little else.

This is having a significant impact on global ecology. There are differing points of view: either we are heading into an apocalyptical abyss or everything is going to be fine. Whatever the answer is, it is clear that we are in uncharted waters. There is no doubt that, overall, human society is having a massive impact on the environment, much of which is negative and destructive. Pesticides, plastics, climate change, melting ice caps, ozone layer, GM crops—there is plenty food for thought. Perhaps time is running out, perhaps it is now or never—or perhaps not. Who knows?

But still our rulers persist in trying to persuade us that everything will be alright and to hang on in there until it is—like when? Blair and Bush and the rest of them talk about how important it is that capitalism comes to Africa, how everything is so great. They talk of agreements on industrial emissions and then don't do anything about it. They talk of the 'trickle down' effect of wealth creation but what I see is more like a trickle up of wealth, from us to them. The simple facts of the case are that in the last 50 years, the gap between the richest 20% of humanity and the poorest 20% has doubled. How do the liberal reformers explain that away when they ask to negotiate with the G8, the World Bank, the International Monetary Fund?

Perhaps they should listen to the words of George Kennan, the American State

Department senior planner who wrote in 1948: "We have 50% of the world's wealth, but only 6.3% of its population. In this situation, our real job in the coming period is to devise a pattern of relationships which permit us to maintain this position of disparity. To do so, we have to dispense with all sentimentality... we should cease thinking about human rights, the raising of living standards and democratisation".

Asking these people—the G8 leaders and the rest of the wealthy elite—to help the poor of the 'developing' world is like asking Hitler to help the Holocaust victims.

This isn't an exaggeration or a clever literary turn—this is the plain and simple truth. There is a silent Holocaust going on in the 'developing' world. We in the 'developed' world are not dying in those numbers but our lives would have so much more potential if only we could break free from the stultifying embrace of capitalism and start to develop a human society that comes to the realisation that we all are from one. A society in which there are no borders, in which the boundaries between ourselves and our environment have been broken down.

It is accepted now by many scientists that at the big bang there was only one atom—in a real and practical sense, we are all from one. If we are to survive and develop our humanity, then that has to be our basis. It is about creating a free and equal society where individuals are able to explore their individuality while at the same time being part of a collective. I believe that this is possible—I know for a fact that change is certain, the question is what kind of change.

If we let them continue murdering our world, then for sure change is going to mean that our lives—the lives of the vast majority of the population—will become significantly harder, if not descending into some cyberpunk apocalypse. If we develop our struggles, strengthen our movements for social justice and world revolution, then who knows—at the very least it is better to struggle on our feet than die on our knees. So, yes, that's why I went to Genoa, that's why I took part in the battle of Genoa. I am against capitalism, I am an anti-capitalist who believes in world revolution.

A non-capitalist society is a society without money, market systems, class divisions, wage labour, commodities—where the things that we require to live are not produced for profit but for self-determined human need, where we are no longer alienated from each other. The fundamental problem with the world is that a loaf of bread isn't produced to be eaten but is produced to be sold at a profit. Everything—even human life—has a price, is a commodity to be bought and sold. Trees are being cut down in the Amazon rainforest not because people don't like them as trees but because they can be sold.

But on to Genoa—when I talk of the battle of Genoa, that doesn't mean that I think that everyone should be out there fighting the police. What I think is that we should all respect each other's tactics in an atmosphere of healthy criticism—our strength is our diversity and certainly in this country too much energy has been wasted on endless violence/non-violence debates. In fact, nowadays I prefer to use the word 'confrontation' rather than 'violence'.

I personally believe that we have to confront the state and its agents, the police—the robocops of capitalism. I certainly don't think that marching from park A to park B will change anything, rather it is just a safety valve that domesticates our dissent. But I do think that singing and dancing and wearing bright clothes and confronting capitalism is just as valid as pulling on a balaclava and throwing rocks at the police—possibly even more valid. As said, our strength is our diversity and we need to recognise and embrace that fact. As the Zapitistas said, one "no" and many "yes": the no to capitalism, the yes to diversity, different paths, variety being the spice of life. Remember that they are the genuine monoculturists, the one crop imperialism of McDonalds, Starbucks, Coca-Cola, Nike: everything the same. We are the multitude of flowers springing through the cracks in the pavement, laughing and dancing and smiling.

So onwards and upwards. Arrive in Genoa and make sure that I know the area. That's a major problem with being in a new city: don't know the geography—and on top of that, it is in a country that I have never visited before. I don't know the language—typical Brit on holiday—and I don't know the popular culture, so to speak. When I say 'popular culture', I mean what the situation is: how the police behave, how the demonstrators behave, what the local people think of things, what the left groups do, what the anarchists do, what are the relationships between the different groups. I know what these are in Britain, I have a sketchy knowledge of Italian politics but that's where it stops. This is an obstacle that came up many times while I was in Genoa and led me to question the validity of crossing Europe to go on a demonstration. Added to that is, of course, the ecological impact of flying, maybe one of the most unecological activities an individual can do (ignoring the vast ecological impact of global capitalism).

I went to a meeting of the 'international Genoa offensive' at a social centre in the city. Hard work at the meeting—everything had to be translated into three

languages and people were talking round and round in circles. There seemed to have not been much preparation and the Italian anarchists appeared not to have made attempts to organise for a specific anarchist block on the day of direct action.

People were angry about this and frustrated as no other group—for example, the radical workers grouping of Cobas, the white overalls and the pinks—wanted the anarchists to be with them as a block on the direct action day. In retrospect, I can understand why (though that didn't stop those groups getting attacked by the police either). I remember one person demanding that we start attacking property now, another condemning the militarism of the black block. Already at least two places had been raided by the police and people were tense and nervous.

As at each meeting there were different people—and the meetings were obviously growing in size as the day of reckoning approached—the same ground had to be gone over and over again. My feeling was that there was a lack of co-ordination and preparation, but then as anarchists we have to depend on ourselves and each other, there are no leaders to tell us what to do as we passively follow like sheep. At the end of the day, despite the difficulties of the meeting, I would rather be an anarchist. At least we are trying to do it ourselves and that's the only way there will ever be genuine social transformation—when we all do it for ourselves.

So day one—the migrants march. I watched the march leave the square: there were thousands after thousands. It had been agreed before that the march was going to be pacifist as there were 'illegal' migrants on it and so there was a need to protect them (I assume that protection also meant that if the police attacked, then the march would resist but that was never made clear, which is a sign of the liberalism of the event and the liberalism of the overall organisers, the Genoa Social Forum). It should also be said that at times it is good to have a march that is pacifist: let us reserve and keep our strength.

There were many anarchists—it must have been the largest number of anarchists that I had ever seen. There wasn't one particular block, they were spread out all over the march. There were great banners and placards, many individually made (always a healthy sign—I hate the dominance of the one placard: the monoculturism of the left like the Socialist Workers Party). I remember one great banner that stated 'you can't forbid it and you can't ignore it, you try to frighten but you will not stop it—the global resistance'. There were some great chants as well—"no justice, no peace/fuck the police" (very common slogan for the next three days), "no borders, no nations/stop deportations", "Genoa libera" (liberate Genoa) and "fight, fight, fight/fight fortress Europe".

As the march went through the streets, there was support from the windows, people waving, cheering. At one point a few things were thrown at the police but people then stood between that and the police—note that amongst the people doing the standing there were anarchists, another example (amongst the millions of examples) to dispel the myth that all anarchists are violent psychopaths. Like everyone else, anarchists are a range of people and the vast majority of them are deeply compassionate and caring individuals who have a great deal of sensitivity for their own situation and the situation of the other people around them.

I heard that there were about 60,000 people on the march—not bad for a Thursday. The police hung back, they didn't actually police the march as they do in this country (another example of cultural differences)—at certain junctions they were standing there looking mean but that was that. After the march, it was make body armour time. I don't know if I had been overdosing on white overall fantasies, but I decided to make some body armour for myself—when in this country, I would not have thought of doing such a thing, I would have concentrated on being light and mobile. In retrospect, I should have stuck with being light and mobile.

Come Friday morning—tension, excitement, fear filled the air. This was the day of reckoning, the day of our rage against the bastards behind their Red Zone. Time for some revenge, time to remove their bloated faces from the media and replace them with demonstrations of our anger. I went with the black block—that dreaded word! In the aftermath of Genoa, the state strategy was clear: to brutally attack and politically divide the movement and part of that division was based on the demonisation of the black block. At the heart of this demonisation is an attack on the idea of confrontation against the state—and an attack on the idea that we don't need leaders, that we can act autonomously, for ourselves and outside the established order.

The black block is primarily an European situation, we don't have one in this country for which personally I am glad—but then maybe the tactic developed in response to the policing strategy or maybe it developed due to the militant isolationism of anarchists in such countries as Germany. I knew that I wanted to physically confront the state and the G8 and I believed that the black block was the best tool for that purpose.

There were enough of us where we were camping to form our own block—during the night, the place had been radically restructured to provide people with ammunition for the coming day's event. Before anyone gets on their high horse about this, let them look at the ammunition of the state: it is not just a matter of body armour and helmets and truncheons and tear gas, it is a matter of police vans, water cannons, rubber bullets, live bullets, concussion grenades, armoured cars, helicopters, tanks, nuclear weapons.

Against that, our sticks and stones look positively puny. I see our weapons as almost being tokenistic, symbolic—it illustrates the depth of our discontent, it demonstrates the fact that we reject that the state's ideological policing of our political activity, it indicates that we recognise the fact that unfortunately some level of violent confrontation will have to be had with the wealthy elite if we are going to achieve our goals of a different world to the one they currently control. But come on—a stone against a helicopter, a stick against an armoured car—and they call us violent?

To be honest, there is no comparison—they are the real butchers, they are the ones whose hands are covered in blood from not only the silent holocaust but from the massacres in Chechnya, the Gulf War, Latin America and many other places.

My violence is less than a fraction of a drop of a water in the entire oceans of the world when compared to theirs and at least I am prepared to be honest about it while they live in a state of constant denial. At the end of the day all we have is our hearts, our minds and our bodies—and I think that a lot more people are going to die before they are forced to give up their privileges and their power. Carlo Giuliani might have been the first person to die in this recent round of anti-capitalist demonstrations in the 'developed' world but plenty have already died elsewhere—like Papua New Guinea where three people were killed in the weeks before Genoa.

It would simply take too long to list all the acts of state violence but the point has to be made that when Blair and Co condemn the violence of the demonstrators, it is time that they had a good long look in the mirror and asked certain questions about their consistency and honesty... but of course asking them to do that is asking the impossible.

At Genoa, even specifically pacifist marches were tear gassed and batoned by the police. I saw later photographic evidence of a cop walking amongst part of the pacifist march that is sitting down, wildly swinging his truncheon and hitting people. Genoa marked an increase in the militarisation of the state, power centralised into an iron fist crushing dissent. Of course, with fortress Europe, what happened in Italy will be happening here—let us not forget the imprisonment of several thousand people on Mayday this year at Oxford Circus for eight hours.

So back to the black block (that sounds like a good hip-hop song—let's get back, back, back to the black block). We move on to the road like some medieval army, mainly dressed in black, masked up, rudimentary ammunition at the ready. Off we go—only one cop in sight, we had been expecting divisions of police, our paranoia had been running on full but where were they? The plan (if you could call it that) was to join the Cobas march and then make our way with them towards the Red Zone and then break off at some appropriate moment and attack the state and exact some payback.

Now my memory starts to go slightly hazy—I am writing this some time after the event, so much happened in such a short space of time and I was literally main-lining adrenalin. As I remember we got down to a square where there were other people and then some individuals from the black block started attacking a bank. From my perspective this was a distraction—people looked at the bank, at those doing the attack and argued with each other.

The crowd that we were seeking to join were probably not overly impressed by these antics—I think that it is a good idea sometimes to control our energy and our rage, to focus it on appropriate targets (not saying that a bank isn't an appro-priate target—obviously it is—but there are times and places) at the right time. We seemed to be standing around for quite a while, during which the bank gets well and truly trashed—next thing is that there are police at the end of a street and the air is full of teargas.

Teargas seems to be everywhere but that might be my mistaken impression due to being tear gassed for the first time in my life. I thought that the Euro-militants would take on the police but the black block quickly fragmented into several different groups and there wasn't a concerted effort to attack the police—a far better though far harder strategy than just doing over a bank.

Perhaps we needed a bit of leadership—there's nothing wrong with leader-ship in specific situations and anarchists have to grasp this thorny issue. Leaders can be temporary, it does not mean they have the right to lead all the time—just at this particular time. There needs to be a structure of affinity groups, delegates and leaders to assist our activity and ensure that we don't get too lost. This structure did

seem to be apparent in the initial organising meetings but not apparent on the actual day (though obviously some groups were working together).

At one point I charged forward, high on adrenalin ready to fight the police— but then a tear gas canister exploded at my feet and everything went strange for a short time and I retreated, my courage undermined by lack of equipment and police activity.

There seemed to be a lot of pointless activity from my perspective—all the bottle bank bins and rubbish trolleys were being dragged into the street and set on fire, the odd car was being burnt out—why? What was the point of it? At times we need to build barricades to defend our territory against the police but a lot of this seemed without direction or much thought past simple chaotic creation. But this can easily backfire—the rubbish bin dragged into the street can stop you getting away from the police, the property destruction can alienate you from the people you wanted to march with.

I think that we all need to carefully consider our actions and try to plan for things rather than running round in a spiral of petty destruction. One of the most stupid incidents that I personally saw was someone with an ice pick... smashing up a telephone box. Myself and others went over to him and he stopped but why had he started in the first place?

As far as the question of police infiltration is concerned, I would have thought that the police definitely did have individuals within the black block—of course, it is easy to mask up and then no-one knows who anyone else is. But the police also have people on the central committee of the Socialist Workers Party, the police also have people high up in the Trades Union Congress, even in the Campaign for Nuclear Disarmament—the police are there. Just because we are infiltrated doesn't mean that our tactics are wrong.

A much more valid criticism of the black block is that by its nature it makes itself separate from other demonstrators, many of whom are just as prepared and just as willing to attack the police. It is almost as though the black block fetishises itself and becomes a symbol of manufactured resistance rather than an act of real resistance. Maybe that's over-intellectualising but what I am trying to say is that the black block cuts itself off from other people who want to get stuck in. We shouldn't be trying to cut ourselves off, we should be involving ourselves as much as possible with other people.

What was surprising for me was the seemingly low level of police intelligence (no sniggering at the back, but they didn't seem to know what was going on) and the definite low level of surveillance. Coming from this country with a CCTV camera on every corner and the Forward Intelligence Team (the police surveillance group) on every demonstration, this was amazing. I think that I saw one camera during the entire time that I was there and that was pointing out of a helicopter.

I wonder if the police infiltrators on the black block (if there were any—but I am assuming that there were some) started the property destruction to distract us from the task of attacking the Red Zone? But I know that there are some people within the anarchist movement who would seize any opportunity to smash up banks and burn out cars at the drop of a balaclava so who knows? Perhaps in terms of overall strategy, the black block should attempt to agree to tactics beforehand and then people who ignore that agreement should be asked to leave the group and form their own blocks.

We then roamed the city, smashing up banks, getting tear gassed, building barricades and looting shops. Personally, I felt a bit pissed off at the looting—another example of a distraction, especially while the Red Zone remains unattacked. But I accept that looting has a place in our actions. Looting can be a powerful symbol of our rejection of property values and a practical form of temporarily meeting needs. And looting can often be more inclusive than streetfighting (you don't need to have a level of physical fitness).

But back to the action. At one point I came across an excellent marching band—lots of drums, right equipment (gas masks or swimming goggles). They were like a band of medieval musicians leading the rebellious peasantry. Yet they lacked support from other people and despite all efforts, people seemed just to mill around without a clear sense of direction (maybe that was because we were all fucking lost). When I got back to this country I saw the marching band used on TV footage with some commentator going on about nazis—they (and this is everyone from the BBC to the SWP) try to vilify the black block as police and nazis but the reality is that the black block are people prepared to have a go at the police and to smash symbols of capitalist wealth. What's wrong with that?

I finally ended up in a square where bizarrely there was a banner from UCATT, perhaps one of the most corrupt and useless unions in Britain and a jazz band—down in the city all hell was breaking loose and in this square people were sitting down, listening to the music and having a nice time. No problem with that apart from its slightly surreal nature. I sat down on a park bench, time for a break from all the hectic effort, give my adrenal gland a rest.

Someone had looted a bottle of wine and there were endless attempts to get the cork out—no joy at all, despite best efforts. Is this the shopkeeper's revenge? Next moment bang bang bang, tear gas everywhere again. Someone wanders past in the fog of tear gas selling *Socialist Worker*—unbelievable. I quickly get up, go over to take a look—the police have moved into the square and are firing tear gas. I heave the full wine bottle at them in a sudden spurt of hatred. I am pretty sure that I missed, much to my disappointment—carried away by the moment. When doing these kind of things you have to be so careful, you have to be so aware but often the energy of this activity (anger, aggression, frustration) is directly against being careful. A contradiction that needs to be considered.

So back on the road, looking for something to do. I could see a huge pall of teargas near the station so I headed off towards there—it's the white overall march (Tute Bianche), a massive march that completely fills the road and has been blocked at the station by the police. As I arrive, stewards are telling the march to go back to Carlini (where they are camped), some people are obeying but some aren't.

I am holding a couple of small stones in my hand—tokens of my rage—and I am grabbed by a steward who starts abusing me in Italian. To get away from his authoritarian attention, I have to drop the stones. The left in Italy is far more combative on an organisational level than the left in this country—but it still has the same tendencies of authoritarianism, that crucial "we'll do it for you" rather than the revolutionary "do it ourselves".

I move down towards the front line and tear gas fills the air. They are firing great big cylinders with fins at the end—if you get hit by one of those buggers, you'll know about it. Heroes and heroines are grabbing the grenades as they fall from the sky and either throwing them back at the police or over onto the railway line. The police advance and then fall back, advance and fall back. A petrol bomb is thrown but it lands short of police lines (the only one that I actually saw thrown all the time I was in Genoa).

There isn't so much hand-to-hand fighting with the police. The tear gas is intense—the police have the tools to survive the tear gas, we don't—or at least, not in their numbers. There's some great graffiti—'peace, love and petrol bombs', 'we must take the kingdom of heaven by storm', 'fuck the police', 'new kids on the black block'. The posh hotel beside the station (Hotel Star Presidente or something like that) is completely shrouded in tear gas and smoke from fires.

One point to note is that many of the front liners are ordinary people, dressed in jeans and T-shirts without that much black clothing amongst them. Obviously people are masked up and have helmets but this seems to be usual for demonstrations in Italy and considering the police behaviour, it's sensible. Stones are thrown, the police advance, bring out the water cannon, we retreat and then come forward again, fuelled by bravado and rage against the police, against the G8, against the shit of this world.

Then they bring out the armoured car—another first for me, never been chased

by an armoured car before. It's low and flat, painted army green as I remember with six wheels. As it moves forward it utters this odd siren type sound. Initially it's kind of exciting but this wears off when suddenly it charges far far beyond where the police had charged before.

One moment they are a long way away, next moment they are right amongst us, batons flailing, fucking hell this is scary, I definitely do not want to meet an Italian cop in this situation, I am running like shit. I hear later that the police strategy had been for a fresh force (ie ones who hadn't been doing anything up until now) to come out and do this huge charge up the road backed up by the armoured car.

Slight tactical error on my part is that I run up the pavement where motorcycles are parked—in the swarm of running people, they are knocked over and immediately people fall on top of them, complete chaos and fear. Somehow I manage to get to my feet and dive down a side street—another mistake as Genoa must win the title of the city with the most dead-end streets. There is a whole load of us, crouched in fear, wondering what the fuck is going on—people try to escape over walls but find out that is blocked as well.

After a while, it seems to be alright to go back onto the road as the police have just advanced en masse. I get back on the main road and decide it's time for me to head home—it's getting on and I'm exhausted. As I'm walking down the road, I bump into a face I recognise. She eagerly recounts her experiences: it's being going off all over the city. She is high on the ecstasy of resistance (but simultaneously sad and scared by its reality as well). Courthouse has been set on fire and even better there was an attempted storming of the prison—what better action than that!

Lufthansa office trashed and sprayed with 'no deportations' (Lufthansa are involved in deporting people from Germany).

The group that she was with has had several major fights with the police and at times fought the police back with stones and petrol bombs. Cops have been caught by pincer movements of demonstrators and have had to flee in terror. But she and her friends have also had to flee in terror at times—a yo-yo experience all around! Endless barricades have been built and more tales of people risking their lives and liberty to challenge the G8 and the whole stinking system. And at least one cop van has been isolated and burnt out. The scale of our activity takes my breath away. We part on good terms.

But then as I head back I hear of the murder of Carlo Giuliani. A sense of rage and fury grips me—the predictions have come true, they have murdered one of us. But it had to happen sooner or later—I thought that someone might die on the J18 demonstration in the City of London and in fact one person was run over by a police van.

And of course three people were shot in Gothenburg only the month before—so yes, it was inevitable but it was only inevitable because of the size and success of the anti-capitalist movement. I feel for Carlo, his friends and his family—a loss of life at the age of 23—but at least he died when he was active, at least he died on his feet. I will remember him and I will treasure him in my heart along with everyone else who have had their lives terminated by this beast of a social system.

I had initially thought of going back to this country after the day of direct action on Friday but with the murder of Carlo, everything had changed. There was no way that I was not going on the demonstration on Saturday, I had to show my solidarity with Carlo and I had to show that I was not intimidated by the Italian state—fuck the police.

So to the next day—there was clear blue sky and hot sun—a day for mourning and a day for rage. There were people everywhere, god knows how many were on the march—150,000 or 300,000, whatever, it was massive. And this was after the state had murdered Carlo on Friday. Their attempt to intimidate us into silence, into staying asleep had failed—failed big time.

Thousands of people had black armbands, there were constant cries of "assassino", large banners proclaiming the same message, hurriedly made with red paint on white sheets. Noreena Hertz, that idiotic academic liberal (she's barely even a 'liberal') said that on the Saturday Carlo's death had already been forgotten. Was she on the same planet as me and everyone else? Although there were a lot of political organisations on the march, there were also many many ordinary people who were on the march, angry and focused.

I walked along the march and then next thing I knew was that tear gas was filling the air again—down at the convergence centre at Piazza Kennedy the police were firing tear gas. I don't know why it started and I didn't see the start but again—as the day before—so many people acted with such heroism and bravery that it is almost unbelievable. I really thought that after Carlo's murder, the police would ease off, almost perhaps back down. The opposite is true. They went in even harder, possibly starting the attack on the demonstration. And then of course there were the events on Saturday night. Those of us with illusions about the state please take note.

The air was full of tear gas, the robocops of capitalism would charge with all their array of armoury and still people resisted. The banks that had been trashed the day before were even further trashed until they were past the point of recognition. Did that used to be a bank there? I would never have guessed. There was building of barricades—more appropriately this time—but the wall of tear gas forced the front line to retreat back down the road.

The march started to go up side streets apart from the ones who wanted to have a pop at the police—after all, this is an international sport, having a pop at the police. Slowly everyone retreated down the coast followed by a wall of tear gas and police. I split off from the front line and went inland to see what was happening—nothing much apart from the police firing tear gas and demonstrators trying to get to the end of the march.

I met up with an Italian family—mum, dad, son—all with crash helmets and masks, come for a family day out. We parted with reminders to be careful and look after ourselves. I then almost by accident came back into the front line which had now been pushed back for maybe one mile down the coast—confusion was in command.

There was a big march ahead of us, seemed to be radical unions and the front line tagged onto its back as it went through side streets. Stewards tried to stop us joining or at least keep a distance between us and them. I could see why in some ways—having the black block/militant front line activists at your back was a bit like having a lighted fuse but it must be said that the police were attacking anyone and everyone in their way. If you were there in their way (which meant being in Genoa to demonstrate against the G8), you got attacked, regardless of political affiliations or colour of clothes.

Next thing I knew was that a police van drove into the march at god-knows-what speed with a cop standing in the turret firing tear gas. Everyone scattered and believe it or not I ended up in another fucking dead end street. This time I decided to crouch down in the undergrowth—a good perspective on insect life—while a helicopter circled overhead. After about one hour I reckoned that it would be safe enough to venture back onto the streets. I could still see tear gas and fires elsewhere in the city but I was done in. Walking through the city was a surreal experience. Examples of working class art dotted the battlefield—burnt out, destroyed cars (some of which looked as though they had been run over by an armoured car and maybe they had).

I went back and got my stuff and got the fuck out of the city—I heard the next morning what had happened that night. The raid on the school and the media centre was an act of terrorism by the agents of the G8 designed to intimidate the anti-capitalist movement. It failed despite what Italians have described as the "night of blood and day of terror". Despite the savage assault that left up to a dozen people severely injured and many others hospitalised, despite the subsequent low level torture and demonising propaganda, this movement has not been driven off the streets.

In fact, if the demonstrations in Italy on the Monday—less than 48 hours after the raid—are anything to go by, it has had the opposite effect: politicising and strengthening hundreds of thousands of people. With the raid on the school, I thought the mask has slipped. The smiling happy face of capitalism, that grinning Ronald MacDonald, has been replaced by the truncheon wielding robocop bent on breaking bones.

Since then I have spent a lot of time thinking about what happened in Genoa and what it means for our tactics and our overall strategies. To state the obvious, we need a revolution. We can't reform the World Bank, however much Bono and Bob Geldof try to persuade us otherwise. How can you negotiate with an insatiable thirst for profit that shows absolutely no signs of slacking despite all the warning signs? The Kyoto Agreement (which was crap anyway) is in the dustbin.

Tony Blair and George Bush both have electoral mandates of 1 in 4 people in their respective countries—that looks fairly weak to me. There is an anti-capitalist movement at the moment that presents significant potential but is very broad, certainly in Genoa (I remember seeing a section of the World Wildlife Fund march past at one point)—but perhaps not so much in this country.

In this country the anti-capitalist movement has emerged from a convergence between radical environmentalists and anarchists, aided by a growing sense of unease amongst some liberal organisations and commentators. It has been joined by left groups, some earlier (Workers Power) than others (the SWP). It doesn't appear to have much bearing within the trade union bureaucracy or the Labour Party but I think that is a very good thing. A genuine anti-capitalist movement would sweep them away.

But what has to be done is getting out into workplaces and communities, getting beyond the activist base and its marginalised periphery. When we do that we

have to accept that everyone is, to greater or lesser extents, marginalised and on the periphery. There is no homogenised working class out there waiting for us to come to them like Moses from the mountain. We are all in this together—anarcho-elitism has the same mindset as Leninist elitism.

Politics has to be made real to everyday life (though how real is everyday life?) and not just dependent on six monthly spectaculars for a political fix. What is important with this movement is that simple phrase 'anti-capitalist'. I remember the first time that the media used it during the J18 demonstration and it was amazing to hear the BBC talk about "anti-capitalism". This information is going out to millions of people in this country and across the world—there is an alternative to this shit, there is something that is anti-capitalist.

But is there a movement? That's a good question. There is a movement of discontent due to perhaps a general awareness that time is running out. People are anxious and worried about where we are going. Alongside acceptance of the trinkets offered to us by capitalism, there is also uncertainty and insecurity.

These are the experiences of many people and I think that the anti-capitalist movement has potential to tap into that popular feeling. We need to be getting our message across as much as possible through all variety of ways: leaflets, stickers, posters, graffiti, internet, e-mail, text messaging, street theatre, talking to neighbours, whatever. Information for action and action for information—questioning, doubting, debating, challenging. Not asking for a few more crumbs but for the whole bloody bakery.

But in that process, we must never turn to armed struggle—this would be complete bollocks and if it wasn't actually state initiated, it would be following the state agenda. Again, it's getting back to "we'll do it for you". As opposed to the mass, open participation of a demonstration or a riot, armed struggle is elitist activity conducted by a small group meeting in secret. This is bullshit—we will all do it for ourselves. So no paramilitary fantasies and if anyone offers you a bomb, tell them to fuck off (and at the same time tell them that they are following the agenda of the state). One conclusion of this type of activity is atrocities like the planes hijacked by suicide bombers crashing into New York and Washington. This indiscriminate terror is just the other side of the coin to the state's indiscriminate terror (like United States attacks on Afghanistan, Iran, Iraq, Serbia, Somalia, its unwavering support for Israel and so on). If we are to get anywhere, it has to be clear that we stand for the fiesta of life against their machines of death.

After Genoa, there was a slogan that 'Genoa is everywhere' and it's true. It's also true that we are all Carlo Giuliani. From our pain and suffering, we need to develop our human solidarity and empathy with each other so that we build a movement that not only overthrows capitalism but creates a society of beauty and adventure. Often our natural compassion is swamped by hatred of what we are against and we end up hating more than loving. Hate can be a toxin that poisons our initial motives for taking action. That's a dangerous path, a path our rulers are only too glad for us to take.

We need to consider our intentions and our motivations. We need to be constantly aware of what they are in order for us to maintain our focus. As has been said, those who talk of revolution without referring explicitly to love are talking with a corpse in their mouth. Our revolution has to spring from love and compassion otherwise it will be doomed.

There are many things that are far more revolutionary than throwing a brick—for example, meditative self-examination or putting out ideas. It could be said that it's easier to chuck a brick than talk to our neighbours but talking to our neighbours can have more value. We cannot take the state on militarily for that is the path to defeat. The state and capitalism can only be overthrown by a tide of working class people acting as a social movement with parallel structures and political analysis. So that means putting out our ideas, one area where I think our movement falls down — propaganda of word is essential.

If we are to have social transformation as opposed to a bloodbath (remembering that in all probability that we would lose a bloodbath), then we need to get more and more people involved. It's about getting our point of view across—the vast majority of people, despite their varied discontents and dissatisfactions, do not actually know what anti-capitalism is.

On the basis of the passion of our imagination, the carefulness of our awareness and the compassion of our love, we can evolve our movement to the point where it swamps the G8 in a sea of people. We are your brothers, your sisters, your sons, your daughters, your lovers, your fathers, your mothers—we are everywhere. Our hearts, our minds, our bodies, they are our only real weapons. For us to get to that time where we have abolished the G8 and all it stands for, we have to look at ourselves. We need to be locally involved, in communities and workplaces, pushing the message that there is an alternative, that a different world is possible, that there is an anti-capitalist movement.

The spectre of revolution is again haunting the capitalist corridors. While capitalism stalks us as consumers at the same time as dumping us as workers, it has the audacity to squeal when we brick its windows. The capitalist empire has never been so dominant as now but empires always collapse.

With the world economy sliding into recession we have the potential to make significant interventions, for we already have a fledgling movement, a movement that expresses a level of discontent that strikes a popular chord. It is about turning a protest movement into a social movement into world revolution for a global human community. I am tempted to end by saying that we have nothing to lose but our trainers but I think it's better to say that we have everything to gain.

> > T W E L V E

what the protesters in genoa want

by MICHAEL HARDT & ANTONIO NEGRI

Genoa, that Renaissance city known for both openness and shrewd political sophistication, is in crisis this weekend. It should have thrown its gates wide open for the celebration of this summit of the world's most powerful leaders. But instead Genoa has been transformed into a medieval fortress of barricades with high-tech controls. The ruling ideology about the present form of globalisation is that there is no alternative. And strangely, this restricts both the rulers and the ruled.

Leaders of the Group of Eight have no choice but to attempt a show of political sophistication. They try to appear charitable and transparent in their goals. They promise to aid the world's poor and they genuflect to Pope John Paul II and his interests. But the real agenda is to renegotiate relations among the powerful, on issues such as the construction of missile defense systems.

The leaders, however, seem detached somehow from the transformations around them, as though they are following the stage directions from a dated play. We can see the photo already, though it has not yet been taken: President George W. Bush as an unlikely king, bolstered by lesser monarchs. This is not quite an image of the future. It resembles more an archival photo, pre-1914, of superannuated royal potentates.

Those demonstrating against the summit in Genoa, however, are not distracted by these old-fashioned symbols of power. They know that a fundamentally new global

system is being formed. It can no longer be understood in terms of British, French, Russian or even American imperialism.

The many protests that have led up to Genoa were based on the recognition that no national power is in control of the present global order. Consequently protests must be directed at international and supranational organisations, such as the G8, the World Trade Organisation, the World Bank and the International Monetary Fund. The movements are not anti-American, as they often appear, but aimed at a different, larger power structure.

If it is not national but supranational powers that rule today's globalisation, however, we must recognise that this new order has no democratic institutional mechanisms for representation, as nation-states do: no elections, no public forum for debate. The rulers are effectively blind and deaf to the ruled. The protesters take to the streets because this is the form of expression available to them. The lack of other venues and social mechanisms is not their creation.

Anti-globalisation is not an adequate characterisation of the protesters in Genoa (or Gteborg, Quebec, Prague, or Seattle). The globalisation debate will remain hopelessly confused, in fact, unless we insist on qualifying the term globalisation. The protesters are indeed united against the present form of capitalist globalisation, but the vast majority of them are not against globalising currents and forces as such; they are not isolationist, separatist or even nationalist.

The protests themselves have become global movements and one of their clearest objectives is for the democratisation of globalising processes. It should not be called an anti-globalisation movement. It is pro-globalisation, or rather an alternative

globalisation movement, one that seeks to eliminate inequalities between rich and poor and between the powerful and the powerless, and to expand the possibilities of self-determination. If we understand one thing from the multitude of voices in Genoa this weekend, it should be that a different and better future is possible. When one recognises the tremendous power of the international and supranational forces that support our present form of globalisation, one could conclude that resistance is futile.

But those in the streets today are foolish enough to believe that alternatives are possible, that 'inevitability' should not be the last word in politics. A new species of political activist has been born with a spirit that is reminiscent of the paradoxical idealism of the 1960s. The realistic course of action today is to demand what is seemingly impossible, that is, something new.

Protest movements are an integral part of a democratic society and, for this reason alone, we should all thank those in the streets in Genoa, whether we agree with them or not. Protest movements, however, do not provide a practical blueprint for how to solve problems, and we should not expect that of them. They seek rather to transform the public agenda by creating political desires for a better future.

We see seeds of that future already in the sea of faces that stretches from the streets of Seattle to those of Genoa. One of the most remarkable characteristics of these movements is their diversity: trade unionists together with ecologists together with priests and communists. We are beginning to see emerge a multitude that is not defined by any single identity, but can discover commonality in its multiplicity.

These movements are what link Genoa this weekend most clearly to the openness toward new kinds of exchange and new ideas of its Renaissance past.

> > T H I R T E E N

trots and liberals

by TOMMY

Some things sometimes need to be said: and what I want to say is about the authoritarian left groups (the trots) and the liberals within the anti-capitalist movement. I apologise in advance for perhaps sounding a bit sectarian but it is just that I have learnt from my past—from before Genoa and at Genoa.

In this country, the largest authoritarian left group is the Socialist Workers Party. The SWP is a typical Trotskyist organisation—it is opportunist and shallow. But this isn't true of many ordinary SWP members.

These ordinary members are excellent to work with, have good politics, are practical and straightforward. They have track records of working well with people from other political backgrounds and they are open to debate and discussion. They have no problems getting stuck in when necessary and indeed it is understandable why they are in the Socialist Workers Party. After all, the party is the largest organisation on the left which can be attractive in itself. The party has a regular weekly newspaper, two theoretical magazines, local groups spread out around the country, large annual conferences, a range of books and is involved in various forms of street activity. The party attracts because it is accessible—a ready-made package.

But ultimately many of these ordinary members leave the party because the party always gets rid of its best members—or they learn to bite their tongues and maintain a level of surface obedience. Within the party there is no real, genuine debate and criticism—surely this must be the lifeblood of any revolutionary organisation? It is a question of whether a person has ideas or whether ideas have the person in an ideological prison of dogma.

Their anti-capitalist front group, Globalise Resistance, claimed in a press release issued after Genoa to be "at the centre of the anti-capitalist movement, bringing together all those who are campaigning against the abuses of capitalism". Who are they trying to con? They claim to be "at the centre of the anti-capitalist movement" but where were they in J18? Friday 18th June 1999: there were up to 15,000 people demonstrating in the city of London on a weekday but the SWP was nowhere to be seen—apart from those ordinary members who had the ability not to be blinkered by the organisation. In terms of institution and hierarchy, the SWP dismissed J18 out of hand... until they saw how successful it was and turned turtle quicker than you could say Trotsky.

But what are they trying to do with this current outpouring of energy? As a Globalise Resistance speaker said in Genoa "Remember, we're the only people here with an overall strategy for the anti-capitalist movement. So I want five people to go out with membership cards, five to sell papers and five to sell bandannas" (SWP/GR meeting, 18th July 2001, Genoa convergence centre). Individuals just become fodder for the party machine, selling papers, building the party. Their claim to be at the centre of the anti-capitalist movement is undermined by the reality of their party: they oppose confronational direct action and they encourage voting for the government.

I believe in anti-capitalist unity—but watering down anti-capitalist politics to gain a spurious 'unity' is a betrayal that history rarely forgives. The in-yer-face, on the streets anti-capitalism is what gives our movement its vitality and attracts support for our activities—it's not something to be played down, disguised or be embarrassed about.

There is much positive common ground between people in the anti-capitalist movement and it is vital that we emphasise this commonality rather than looking for divisions. But when people's resistance and revolutionary desire is expressed through groups like the SWP and GR, that commonality is undermined by the institutional mentality—the existing or potential unity can evaporate in a flood of blinkered party building.

The SWP have become involved in the anti-capitalist movement for different reasons to many others. Their main aim is to take control of the anti-capitalist movement and turn it into an ineffective, pro-Labour pressure group so as to increase the influence and membership of the SWP. They are not primarily interested in working with others—they fundamentally disagree with the politics of just about everyone else involved.

And they are trying to do this through Globalise Resistance. It is only interested in activities to the extent that its brand recognition increases. Globalise Resistance acts radical without actually acting radically. They present an image of resistance which has little concrete substance. It is more a matter of consumption—the book, the bandanna, the counter-conference, the membership card—than a matter of self-determined participatory involvement. At a recent meeting they had a stall above which proclaimed a banner saying "Join GR and buy stuff here". It was almost as though that was the limit of their actual activity.

Commenting on Gothenburg, GR's full-time organiser said, "GR has gone down brilliantly, the words on the GR banner 'People before Profit, Our World is Not for

Sale' were taken up and chanted by the whole protest!" Globalise Resistance would no more take part in an action without prominently displaying its banners and plac-ards than an oil company would give money to an environmental project without telling anyone. The important business of their countrywide tour was reported in *Socialist Worker*: "On the Globalise Resistance tour 18 people joined the SWP in Manchester, 10 in Birmingham, 9 in Sheffield, 8 in Leeds and 4 in Liverpool".

But these tactics are not new to the SWP. It was the same in the anti-poll tax movement in 1990/91 and the anti-fascist movement in the 1970s to name just two examples. The SWP now claim that the Anti-Nazi League (another SWP front group) smashed the National Front off the streets in the battle of Lewisham in 1977—in fact, the Anti-Nazi League was set up several weeks after the battle of Lewisham. But there were many ordinary members there who defied the party line and got stuck in.

During the campaign of mass resistance to the poll tax in the late 1980s/early 1990s, the SWP insisted that only the unions would be able to beat the tax. Dismiss-ing the mass non-payment movement in Newcastle, for example, they said "in a city like Newcastle the 250 employees in the Finance Department are more powerful than the 250,000 people who have to pay the poll tax". If the SWP had had their way, there would have been no non-payment campaign and the poll tax would not have been defeated.

But what most clearly differentiates the institution of the SWP from anyone with a spark of anti-capitalism is their support for the Labour government. The SWP have always voted for the Labour Party. At the last election they stood Socialist Alliance candidates in a minority of seats but instructed their members to vote Labour in the majority of seats. In one publication they described a vote for Labour as "a vote for continuing inequality, poverty, privatisation and slavish devotion to the market" (*IS* 90, p100) yet earlier on in that very same publication they had announced that "our approach in the coming election should be 'vote Socialist where you can, vote Labour where you must'"(*IS* 90, p14).

The SWP would have us believe that the Labour Party and trade union bureau-cracies are full of closet anti-capitalists who can hardly wait to take to the barricades —as long as we behave ourselves and make them welcome. When they tell us that "many who were on the anti-capitalist demonstrations or sympathised with them will also be members of the Labour Party" and "trade unionists are natural enemies of corporate power" you know that they're not calling on trade unionists to adopt direct action—they are trying to convince anti-capitalists to tone down their activities so as not to upset these people. Too many people have an outdated view of trade unions, confusing what they used to be—defenders of some sections of the working class against the worst ravages of capitalism—with what they are today—big bus-inesses trying to defend their markets by selling credit cards and cheap car insur-ance.

When they write that "combining direct action with electioneering will not always come naturally to those from a Labour background" (*IS* 90 p33) you know it's not the electioneering that will be quietly forgotten as they try to dissolve the anti-capitalist movement into a sad left-wing pressure group.

What I would say to SWP members is look at your party, the institution, the

hierarchy, its politics (for example, without sounding too boring, what it says about the brutal repression of the workers' uprising in Kronstadt in 1921)—and then think for yourself, make your own decisions, reject this 'received' politics and take your own way. Really, why bother with the Labour Party and trade union bureaucracy? What's the point? The dinosaurs have died, revolutionary politics need to move on—but the Trotskyist ideology seems to be as stuck as was the Stalinist ideology. But Stalinism is dead, social democracy might be dying and Trotskyism is unwell.

Revolutionary politics needs to be genuinely revolutionary (and this goes for anarchism as well, often stuck in the 19th century, troubled by bitter sectarianism and inbred group loyalism). The SWP is not interested in the anti-capitalist movement, it is only interested in hoovering up what it considers to be the 'best' activists and then moving on to something else. For all its talk and all its placards, what has the SWP actually done, what has it actually initiated (apart from lobbying the Labour Party)?

The SWP is parasitical. It is far more interested in building alliances with reformist organisations such as the Green Party and Jubilee 2000, promoting liberals such as George Monbiot and Susan George than in working with other revolutionaries (I wonder why?). It is social movements that change society, not political parties—the anti-capitalist movement has the potential to become a great force for change and it could become even greater if members of the SWP threw their membership cards into the dustbin of history and actively joined in the movement.

The same goes for liberals who think that things can be made slightly better, life can be improved without all this radical sounding nonsense. Take a look at the statistics, see the reality of the situation. Analyse the society in which we live and make your pain at what is occurring into a force for positive change—embark on a process of alchemy!

Asking capitalism to reform itself fundamentally so that it is providing for the majority of the population and not destroying the planet is a waste of time—it's not possible and it will not happen. There might be more 'green' products (but who owns the 'green' companies?), there might be a greater choice of 'organic' vegetables but the heart of the beast beats on. The wage economy, the market, money still rule our lives. People of a liberal persuasion often have some of the right ideas but are too frightened to take those steps towards an anti-capitalist perspective. It is scary, it can be so much easier having compartments of 'single issues', believing that Christian Aid and Oxfam are doing some good, hoping against hope that things will somehow be made better by someone else. But no issues are single, charitable institutions are at best only smoothing the very rough edges of capitalism (wouldn't it be more efficient to actually do away with capitalism?) and ultimately only we can make things better.

It is hard taking steps at times and it is not as though anarchism has all the right answers. Anarchists and anarchism have made plenty of mistakes throughout history but have generally been much more able to openly discuss them and not get tied down by the baggage of ideology—like the trots—or fear of confronting the whole machine—like the liberals. Many good people have come from liberal and trot backgrounds (and many good people still have liberal/trot ideas): take a look at what is around you and make up your own minds. I know that taking the first step isn't easy but then we have to dare to dream, we have to dare to step outside the established boundaries.

from movement to society

by M A S S I M O   D E   A N G E L I S

E ver since Seattle, and above all in the months leading up to Genoa, two main issues have been raised in an effort either to delegitimise the movement, or else to force it on to the defensive. These are the issues of 'violence' and of 'alternatives'. In both cases, we are called upon to take a clear position, to draw lines in the sand, to define, to classify and to be precise. In the first case, our failure to do so is portrayed as an ambiguity that disguises possible collusions with violent or 'criminal' behaviour, thereby paving the way for the criminalisation of the entire movement. In the second, our failure to assume a clear position is portrayed as a lack of serious intent in dealing with the problems of the world.

By and large, the movement as a whole has refused so far to accept these fronts as legitimate, at least in the terms posed by its opponents. To call for the marginalisation and repudiation of the 'violent' fringes in our movement, on an *a priori* ethical ground that defines this or that as the only legitimate form of struggle, would be to introduce in the movement a serious element of division. It would also show an utter indifference to the social basis of that form of struggle, as well as, in different context, its historical strength and value. On the other hand, to try to unify the movement on the basis of a comprehensive programme which alleges to be an 'alternative' would be not only to render millions of different voices of this movement silent. It would also delegate to a new political hierarchy the sole role of defining for the rest of us what

we do want. The movement's inclusive, horizontal character and profoundly democratic spirit has saved it from all-encompassing manifestos that would close off
demands and therefore open them to co-optation by neoliberal capital.

But Genoa is a turning point. The level of confrontation chosen by the Italian
branch of the Empire's police is without precedent for a country that proclaims itself
a democracy. Blood has been spilled, the young life of Carlo Giuliani taken, and intim-
idation, torture and beating made the rule. Genoa poses the question of 'what do
we do next?' with impressive urgency. Several issues are at stake. The debate has
exploded worldwide on the internet and on other media. The wave of criminalisation
has acquired momentum, and the movement must reinvent itself. In this piece I
argue that to avoid entrapment by our opponents, the question of 'violence' and
'alternatives' must be approached together but in different terms from those posed
by our opponents. I believe this is not simply a contingent question of tactics, but a
question of envisaging the political horizon within which our more contingent and
concrete tactics and strategies must be shaped in the months that follow. Dealing
with the issue of 'violence' and 'alternatives' together means that we must make a
leap in the understanding of our movement: not simply as a means to an end, but as
a social force constituting a new society.

ALTERNATIVES

The question of alternatives has been posed from many quarters, including government representatives and neoliberal opinion leaders (see for example the *Economist*,
UK development secretary Claire Short, etc.), as well as from representatives of mass
popular organisations. Indeed, many within the left tradition, including many trade
union leaders, have difficulty understanding this movement. They are puzzled—if
not irritated or threatened—by the network-form of this movement. Many remain
perturbed that the participants in this movement do not take this network-form as an
expression of the low degree of development of the movement, as an early stage in
the process of building a political party better suited to 'represent' the aspirations
of millions. Such observers are disturbed that, on the contrary, the network-form is
taken to be a symptom of strength by movement participants. Many such observers
cannot rid themselves of their suspicion of a movement that does not pose the question of the alternatives to the market in recognisable terms. That is, in terms of a
programme which can be packaged, discussed through the official media channels
within 30 seconds of an average interview, and deliverable to official institutions. Of
course, this is only partially true, as there are many demands on the ground that
represent substantial policies which spring out of the movement (whatever their
limitations, there is the Tobin tax, debt cancellation etc.). But what is generally understood here by alternative is not so much alternative policies on specific issues, but
rather visions of our human sociality on this planet that are alternative to those
conceivable within the framework of the capitalist market. In short, they want
this movement to come out so they can pin us down. The neoliberal bloc want us
to spell out our vision of alternatives to the capitalist market, if we have one. They can
then show that we are either naive in terms of our reforms on the market (see ideas
like 'fair' price, 'fair' profit, 'fair' trade etc., which essentially do not understand the

competitive laws of the market), or else want the 'inefficient' and long-discredited 'state' once again to manage economic affairs (at the cost of individual freedom of choice). On the other hand, those left-wing activists whose tradition is still rooted in a project of alternative based on the state would share with the neoliberal bloc their doubt about reforms of the market, while wanting us to come out in defence of the state. In short, they both want the movement to come out with an alternative to the capitalist market that is posed in recognisable and familiar terms.

From the perspective of social change, the dichotomy between state and market has always framed the debate over alternatives. State is understood as the space of central authority (in whatever form), and market is understood as the space of dispersed human interaction. If the latter creates injustice, political power can then readdress such injustice. If this is true, then it is clear that the party-form becomes a necessity. In other words, if the alternative to the market becomes the state, then the state as we know it requires political parties, or at least organised coherent groups able to put pressure on them. If ultimately the alternative to the market is the state, and the alternative to the state is the market, then the movement's aspirations cannot be properly channeled by its present network-form. If this movement does not see itself as evolving into a twentieth century-style party, how can the alternative to the market occur? After all, those party forms, beyond any difference between reformist or revolutionary political methodologies, had as an aim the conquest of state power. In terms of the social coordination of human activity, it is precisely state power that seems to pose itself as the only alternative to the market.

Incidentally, one cannot object from within our movement that we do not intend to abolish the market, but only to institute some limit by means of 'just' prices and 'just' profits. In the market, the 'justice' of a price and a specific profit is given by the competitive mechanism. If we believe that there is another concept of justice that has nothing to do with the competitive mechanism, then we are told that we must rely on central state authorities to fix this price and enforce it. In other words, if we believe that all that is demanded by this movement is the enforcement of 'proper' prices and 'proper' profits, then the contradiction between the horizontal network-form of this movement and the centralised aspect of modern political processes is plain to see.

However, in asking what this movement 'wants', those on both the 'left' and the 'right' help to reveal a fundamental contradiction between our way of organising ourselves in this movement, and the current way of organising social cooperation, whether through the market or the state. Under the pressure of criminalisation, a process that has been accelerated with the Genoa events, this contradiction may lead our movement to a divisive impasse. Some of its clusters may be pushed to accept the view of our opponents, moderating their organisational forms, disconnecting with the rest of the movement and becoming simply a 'pressure group' or a political party. Once again, the only alternative to the market appears to be the state. Other parts of the movement may just run out of steam and retire into private life. Criminalisation imprisons and tortures bodies, but also souls. In the face of a mounting criminalisation campaign, the question of alternatives is more than an academic question: it is a question about the kind of world we want to live in.

As it happens, we don't need to accept the false opposition between state and market. So far, the movement as a whole has not. From this movement emerges instead the concept and practice of network, horizontality, democracy, of the exercise of power from below, and of rights like those of access to social resources beyond the market and of people's mobility in a world without barriers. All this leads to a vision of 'economic' action that goes beyond either the market or the state. To recognise this, we must take this movement in its entirety, not as 'no global', but as 'no global capitalism'. We can do this if we reflect for a moment on the objective global network dynamics of solidarity and circulation of struggles, rather than on what any particular exponent of the movement has to say. From this perspective of the whole emerges a heterogeneous movement posing the question of limit to the capitalist market. This concept of limit is different from the one of 'just price' or 'just profit' that some are campaigning for. The line that this movement as a whole is drawing in the sand is against growth for growth's sake, as a panacea for the solution of all the evils of the world. To downplay this aspect of the movement is, in my opinion, a big mistake. In Seattle the slogan was 'no new round, WTO turn around'. Notice that the slogan was not saying 'enough' to this or that liberalisation. A new trade liberalisation round would have opened the road to the intensification of competition in sectors like that of services, and to the commodification of new sphere of life. To demand that there be no such round, therefore, meant to pose the question of a limit upon a social system of production that, as Marx would say, is inherently without limit. This is the true contradiction within which we can pose the question of alternatives: the limit to the inherently limitless drive to accumulation. The same happened in a pervasive way through the numerous battles of the last two decades, especially in many countries of the Third World (for example the many 'IMF riots'). These battles have multiplied against privatisations, against SAP, against cuts to social spending, against new enclosures undertaken in every sphere of social life by large capital and its agencies, against a relation with 'nature' that sees the latter only as an economic resource.

This push to place a limit upon the dynamic of capital as a whole has its own ambiguities, especially if we analyse specific positions within the universe of the movement. Even more, perhaps it is precisely because of the ambiguities and contradictory positions between its different components that the movement, taken as a whole, is able to pose the question of a limit to capital accumulation. And this has an important consequence: posing the question of the limit to capital means simultaneously posing the question of the limit that capital places upon human free enterprise (yes, free enterprise—free, that is, from the restrictions of property and rent positions in the capitalist market!). Let's take for example the question of debt. Everyone within the movement is for debt abolition (and here there are of course numerous partial positions that dispute how much of this debt must be abolished, and the forms of the debt cancellation). But in any case, we all agree that the resources thus freed from the suffocation of debt do not represent the alternative. Rather, they are one of its fundamental conditions. "You try," a Nigerian woman told us at the Genoa Social Forum in the days before the police butchery, "to manage a class of 15 students with $50 a year." This is the key issue behind the question of alternatives: not so much income redistribution, but access to social resources beyond the logic of the market, an access that poses the question of another-management of the social relation of production. Remember Marx's question about access to the means of production? And the same is true for a variety of other struggles: that for social services (from Bolivia to UK), for land (i.e. MST in Brazil), that against GMOs (from India to Europe), against enclosures of knowledge represented by patents on pharmaceutical products (Africa), for the right to live in a relation of respect with nature, etc. All these struggles pose the question of the limit to growth for its own sake, and that of a non-commodified access to social wealth. The powerful of the earth are afraid of these limits and questions that are even now spreading across the planet, permeating many social spheres in the process. It is for this reason that they deploy police that intimidate, massacre, and torture. But if we are able to free social resources, how can we then utilise them? The question of the limit to capital as a condition for alternatives opens up that of the forms of such alternatives might assume.

The historical challenge before us is that the question of alternatives (I intentionally use the plural) not be separated from the organisational forms that this movement gives itself. The idea that means and ends, objective and organisational forms, must be kept separate is a common mistake. In the past, it has led to a tragic dissonance between the 'party' and the 'new society' promised by political action. While the former was meant to marshal the masses; the latter designated its future objective. In the mean time, the real aspirations of millions of social subjects would prove incompatible with the party's tactics, and had to be subordinated to the end of reaching an objective posed by an élite. Here we need only think of the history of communism and socialism, which is filled with the marginalisation of women, blacks, gays and lesbians, of repressed grassroots workers and peasants who would not submit to the party directives. Today this model is refused en masse by the movement, which is characterised instead by the desire for respect, dignity, grassroots democracy and exercise of real power. To ask, 'what does this movement want?' as many have done, is to demand the multitude to provide its 'line', its future objective. It is a question that at best empties this movement of content, and at worst forces it to accept the content of our opponents stuck in the dichotomy of state versus market. Instead, we should look at how the multitude organises its differences in order to know what it wants in practice, and how it practises what it wants. And it is here that we need to dig, enquire, analyse, but also, and especially, participate. The crucial question then becomes: up to what point is it possible today to organise social cooperation in forms that reflect our organisational practices, our horizontality and networks? Think of the production of the various counter-summits held in recent years (the last of which that of Genoa), the production of the various Zapatista *encuentros*. Think of the many social practices that produce use values beyond economic calculation, beyond the competitive relation with the other, inspired instead by practices of social and mutual solidarity. All these are modes of coordination of human activity that go beyond the capitalist market and beyond the state. It does seem that we are talking about another world. Indeed, not even the slogan on T-shirts in Genoa was entirely correct: another world is not only possible. Rather, we are already patiently and with effort building another world—with all its contradictions, limitations and ambiguities—through the form of our networks.

Our organisational forms are of primary importance: not so much for reaching a goal external to them, but as a social force that constitutes new forms of social cooperation beyond the capitalist market. To understand this better, we need to understand that the world of capital is also made up of networks. Within the capitalist form of social cooperation, we are forced to relate to each other as competitors, as social subjects who interact in networks. There is, however, a twofold difference. In the first place, the networks of capital deny us any say in defining our relation to the other. Indeed, here the other is an invisible subject, deaf and dumb, replaced by that abstract mechanism which is the market. Here social relations appear as they are, as material relations between people and social relations between things, as Marx put it in his analysis of commodity-fetishism. This is a network-form of social relations with the other based on systematic and continuous competition as an end in itself. From an existential point of view, such relations are utterly meaningless. And it is precisely this interaction that has been intensified in recent years, by absorbing new spheres of social action. On the contrary, those participating in the 'no global capitalism' network movement, with its horizontally-linked clusters, have shown that their driving desire is to practice other human relations. That is, human relations different from those based on the endless competitive work in every sphere of life, relations that turn the 'other' into a de-humanised thing. In any case, the market is not that spontaneous mechanism extolled by Hayek, the champion of the modern neoliberal project. On the contrary, the state and its repressive apparatus provide the very conditions for the market's existence, operation, and protection: capitalist horizontality

ends here. The networks with which the market is protected and enforced are utterly militaristic and vertical in form. In this sense, there is much to learn from recent events in Genoa (as from the daily acts of repression that are widespread in many Third World countries).

Read within the movement's social practice, including the interaction between its internal differences, the dichotomy between state and market (state as central authority, market as sphere of social cooperation) is a false opposition. In the web of this global movement, social cooperation dictates its rules through grassroots democracy, consensus, dialogue, and the recognition of the other. On the other hand, these norms in turn define the modality of social cooperation. 'Authority' and 'social cooperation' stand in a fluid relation, as in a mechanism of feedback: not dictated from outside, but self-constituted through interaction. Hayek believed in the market as the mechanism that, precisely because of the abstract character of its rules, allowed individual freedom. The freedom of Hayek's man was a freedom to choose from a menu that was pre-given by an abstract mechanism. This mechanism, in other words, was external to the concrete character of the individual; indeed, historically it was posed with force by the state. The freedom of women and men in this movement is a freedom that wants to select the menu itself, because life is not abstract, but very concrete. This movement therefore tends to embrace the battle for freedom, taking it away from those neoliberal lies that see freedom only as a freedom of choice by fragmented and isolated individuals who have no say over the rules of their interaction.

The road is therefore of necessity a contradictory one, because in order to have everybody agreeing, everybody must abandon themselves in the recognition of others.

But what is that 'association of free producers' dreamed of by Marx if not precisely this process of mixing and blending?

The movement 'no global capitalism' therefore opens two interdependent fronts. One is that of the limit to capital, and therefore against the limit that capital places upon us. This is the front of access to social resources beyond capitalist market. The other is that of relations with the other, a network based on respect, dignity, and direct democracy. The first poses the question of the commons (in opposition to the enclosures underlying the commodification of spheres of life). The other poses the question of community: or in the words of Marx's *Economic and Philosophical Manuscripts* of 1844, of the communal being, for whom the other becomes a need. Commons and community: is it the case that this movement, once it is taken as a whole, is—without knowing it, or draping things in meta-narratives—posing the question of communism for the twenty-first century?

VIOLENCE

Because of its characteristics discussed above (network, democracy, consensus), it becomes problematic to pose the question of 'what does this movement want?' from outside it. What in practice this movement has shown it wants is horizontality and participatory democracy. Precisely for this reason, asking the question from inside the movement is practical and relational, and part of the process defining norms and sociality. The question of 'what do we do next?' or 'how do we deal with this or that problem?' cannot be addressed purely instrumentally with an economistic mindset which looks for the 'most efficient ways' to reach 'goals' and 'objectives'. Without wanting to idealise the practices of this movement, its network-form—built on decades of struggles of a variety of subjects that have reclaimed respect, dignity and autonomy—is forcing its participants to blur the distinction between means and objectives. There is, in other words, a growing sense that this movement is turning into a community, or, better, into a network of communities. The movement of the movements, or the network of the networks, as this movement has been dubbed, could also be named the community of the communities. Indeed, only by understanding this movement as community of those who fight for a better world that we can properly frame the challenges in front of us.

One of the challenges facing our movement is the danger of criminalisation. Criminalisation occurs when the heterogeneous practices of a movement are turned into a homogeneous mass of 'criminal' behaviour, its aspirations and dreams, turned into criminal plans, its living diversity, into an amorphous blob. This is not a question of whether or not the movement undertakes illegal actions. Criminalisation of a movement has little to do with the breaking of the law. Breaking of the law may well be 'legitimate', as the civil disobedience tradition reminds us, or when it is an open mass practice. Criminalisation occurs when a wall is successfully built between the movement and the rest of society. Criminalisation occurs when fear and confusion is so pervasive that women and men who were about to join the convivial breeze of a new world go back to their room, their flats, their houses, their huts, their holes and shut the doors for the next twenty years. Criminalisation occurs when repression is successfully deployed in order to prevent the movement to turning into society, to prevent its aspirations polluting everyone's dreams and actions. In this respect, there is no doubt that sooner or later, in one form or another, there will be attempts to criminalise the movement.

Criminalisation begins with seduction. Listening to official government declarations, one might believe that they agree with the reasons of protest, while being critical of the methods employed. Government and bank officials, they tell us, are as concerned as the rest of us about the dying children, the disappearing forests, the destroyed livelihoods. It is for this reason, they say, that they meet and agree to create more markets and to promote more competition. For this reason, they say, summits ought not to be disrupted, because the official representatives (regularly elected by not more than 20% of the confused population having a right to vote) are working for the good of all. They agree with the problems, but are not sure about our methods. 'Violence' can always found hidden in methods that do not recognise the ways of official authority. The mark of being 'violent' is always branded on those who are different, while normalised violence remains invisible.

We do not need to repeat that they are trying to criminalise a movement by using the discourse of violence, bending it to their advantage, with the help of media-produced stupidity that suits their image of our movement. We don't need to repeat that the current daily state of affairs is itself violent in the way that it robs million of food and water, of health and access to the legacy of human knowledge enclosed by patents and suchlike. We don't need to repeat that those daily rules enforced by laws and stupid traditions that forces humanity in a continuous rat race for survival, when indeed its warehouses, intelligence, knowledge and resources are so rich and wealthy that to continue running in competition with each other thus artificially creating scarcity is just plain stupid. No, according to them, all these horror stories are the norm: what's violent, rather, is the breaking of windows belonging to multinational banks (which represent branches of the international strangling machine called debt).

No, we don't need to repeat all this: others have done it better. But the issue of 'violence' cannot be brushed aside simply because they are exercising it much more than us. Institutional violence holds the power of judgement, and the power of judgement holds us in contempt to the norms of this society. Had we been able to tear down peacefully, without harming anybody, the walls of shame erected in Genoa by the G8 oligarchy, we would still have been called violent. Instead, in Genoa an urban battle erupted outside the red zone, at the cost of several commercial banks, insurance, travel agencies, sex shops and cars. Is this right? Is this wrong? The debate within the movement risks to degenerate and oscillate between this polarity, a polarity enforced by our opponents. They are trying to criminalise the movement, by asking it to 'isolate' and even 'denounce' the 'violent' window-breakers. A frame of mind constrained between good and evil, is a frame of mind that searches for innocents and sinners according to an impossible and de-contextualised above part criteria, and therefore scapegoats, in this case, the so called 'black bloc'.

Instead, we need to deal with this issue beyond good and evil. Again, it's not a question of the opportunity or otherwise, the ethical correctness or otherwise of destroying a window, but rather whether that action was a responsible action in that context. The question of responsibility, then, is the key question we need to address.

Responsibility is above all a relationship to the other, one that presupposes the belonging in a community.

Thus, let us take briefly the case of Genoa. To talk about 'violence' in Genoa, is actually to talk about the police. Walter Bello calls this 'a police riot'. And like him, I don't think that it 'is appropriate to denounce people who say they are on our side but with whom we may have disagreement over tactics.' But criticism must be made over what Bello calls the 'parasitical tactics' that have emerged in Genoa by several people belonging to the heterogeneous group labelled 'black bloc' (Bs) (incidentally, following Starhawk, it would be more appropriate to refer to 'clusters' than 'blocs').

Parasitical tactics arise when for example groups in this cluster 'would stay at the edges of the march and from there provoke the police by throwing rocks at them.' The police then find the excuse to charge the demo. Walter Bello's approach to this issue is to make our large demonstration 'more organisationally effective in communicating our message to the world', through the organisation of people for 'orderly retreats, swifts advances and disciplined resistance.' He then proposes a strategy to neutralise the 'Bs' problem. This strategy is composed of essentially two main aspects: 1) 'initiate dialogue in the planning for the mobilisation with the more open, honest, and trustworthy B groups with the intent of getting them to agree to respect the political and ethical parameters of our mass actions', and 2) establish 'a series of non-violent measures of suasions and methods of restraining and defusing violent behaviour.'

Bello's approach has the advantage that it does not moralise the question of smashed windows and 'violence'. His position is not one concerning the ethics of smashing the windows of multinational banks, but rather of the safety and respect of the people participating in the demo. But Bello's position does not go far enough. It recognises a more 'trustworthy' section within the Bs, but risks considering even these components of the Bs as 'other', as alien to the movement. He wants to engage them in a dialogue to make them 'agree to respect the political and ethical parameters of our actions'. The questions, however, involve more than this: are there grounds for a two ways communication between the 'Bs' and the others? Are there grounds to define the 'violent' and the 'non-violent' as both part of the same community? Can trust be built among these clusters, as well as mutual respect? Can both agree to respect the 'ethical and political parameters' of their respective actions? Can they both engage in a debate over strategies, and not dividing over their differences in perceiving good or evil? Is it possible to coordinate actions so as each cluster, each affinity group, recognise the others and is responsible towards them? The answer is certainly a disarming 'no' if 'parasitical tactics' become the norm in our demos, and if the reaction to them by the other sections of the movement is one that follows the model in the immediate aftermath of Genoa, when the 'Bs' were simply dismissed by many as 'provocateurs', 'imbeciles', even 'fascist'.

The first commentaries of TV scenes of street battles, burned cars and shops, attributed the 'violence' on the ground both to this bloc of 'bad' people (how many of them? 1000? 2000? 5000? the media started to do some crazy guesswork on their numbers) and to the hundred of thousands of others who 'protected them'. What an original plot for criminalisation, the ugly violent rioter hidden among the accomplices, i.e. everybody having reasons to protest! It took few days to notice that it was precisely because the 'Bs' were not a 'bloc', precisely because they failed to coordinate their action, that some irresponsible groups engaged in 'parasitic tactics'. And it took some days to emerge that the mass street battles with the police erupted in self-defence on the side of the demonstrators included forces from all sections of the demo. The speakers of the Global Social Forum found thus themselves in an impossible position, squeezed between official media and institutional demands that they condemn 'violence' and the multitude's anger at police brutality that cannot conceive 'violence' out of a specific context. Constrained within the logic of 'good' and 'evil', the media-conscious speakers were trapped and started to defend themselves by asking the wrong, damn wrong, questions: 'why did the police allowed the black block to run riot?' (Also, because they were not a 'bloc', they were small groups of people, they were mixed with the other, and nobody, including the speakers of the Global Social Forum, would have allowed the police inside peaceful demonstration to arrest people dressed in black!). 'Why didn't they stop them at the borders?' (Also, because we, the movement, including the speakers of the Global Social Forum, campaigned heavily for free circulation, we fought for this right, and still do. Because we don't want people to be stopped at the border for being dressed in black—or in any other colour for that matter—or for carrying Swiss Army knives, or for wearing ear or nose piercing). This of course does not mean that we should not ask questions regarding the possible collusion of interests, from a historical and strategic perspective, between the state's needs for criminalisation and the acceleration of 'violence' on the ground. It only means that the movement cannot collude with the police and the state to 'condemn' the 'Bs' because the social force constituting this movement also includes this people.

No, if there is an adjective that can define the groups who endangered the demo with 'parasitic tactics', it is irresponsible. Irresponsibility is not a light criticism, precisely because it presupposes their inclusion in our struggle. You can be (ir)responsible only towards your community, not towards some outside force or some grand ethical concept. You cannot be irresponsible without defining its context. And if you are irresponsible towards the 'other' in your community, then think twice, because the world we are fighting against is based precisely on this persistent indifference to the other. And if you keep persisting in being irresponsible, if you continue to refuse to engage and continue to isolate yourself, you will cut yourself from the rest. If you think ghettoisation is what a new world is about, well, we really do have different worldviews, and maybe after all we are not part of the same community.

But if we are part of the same community, if we both think that a new world is one defined by dignified relation to the other, than this movement must understand the practice of responsibility. The latter cannot be posed from the outside, but can only come from within the community. Responsibility, the recognition of the 'others' within the community and therefore the willingness to engage with them, is the way to neutralise the strategy of criminalisation. It is also the basis for our community to reach out to those spheres of society still untouched by our dream of 'another world'.

The 'Blacks,' the 'pinks,' the 'whites,' and the 'reds' (that is everybody who share the tactic pursued by them) must engage in a dialogue with each other, because we are all part of the same community (community of communities). For that reason we need to talk about the value of everybody's actions not simply as a means to reach a goal, but in terms of a means of engagement to the other. Only after we have done this, can we talk about suasion and method to neutralise violence in specific contexts as Bello argues.

It's not only those who believe in 'violent' tactics must understand the practice of responsibility: the 'non-violent' must do the same. If the cost of being 'media-friendly' is to accept the media-representation of social forces (for example, the 'Bs' as a bloc, rather than a loose cluster of European youth with their own aspirations, history, dreams, motivations, emerging out of the community desert produced by 20 years of neoliberal policies); if the cost of being 'media-friendly' is to be trapped in the logic of de-contextualised ethics, which dangerously favours the game of criminalisation of the whole movement, then it is better to reduce our dependence on the media. After all, we do have independent communication channels. In Genoa, TV official reporting was forced to acknowledge the truth of police brutality after indymedia videos, pictures and text accumulated on the web. On that occasion, the alternative production of information infiltrated official channels that, in competition with each other, relied on the mass production of images and stories storming the web. After all, the message to the 'masses' circulates better with the daily work of persuasion and dialogue on the job, in the neighbourhoods, in schools, hospitals, churches and streets than in the living rooms in which we swallow in isolation the stupidity of spineless entertainers. After all, a new world is built through new social relations,

and these require an active participation that is a bit more engaged than TV zapping.

All sides of this large and heterogeneous movement must engage in reflection. Both 'non-violent' and 'violent' risk missing the key point that historically, the rigid contraposition between violence and non-violence belongs in the realm of our opponents. It is they who, by denouncing 'violence' without qualification and context, are able to use it in their chosen contexts. It is they who—history teaches—infiltrate our movement and collude with fascist organisations to amplify and accelerate the use of violence, hoping then, out of a climate of terror and confusion, to implement their message of state 'non-violence' by escalating violent state repression on the entire movement through criminalisation. The rigidities of dogmas always lead to rigid consequences.

Both 'non-violent' and 'violent' positions must come to terms with each other without buying into the rigidities of our opponents, rigidities that are instrumental to the continuation of the truly violent logic of this world. El Viejo, from the PGA network, puts the question of flexibility in this way:

"How is that the Blacks can find themselves doing the same things as police provocateurs? To me, it is because many of them have mystified violence (as many of us did in the '70s). Mystified, it becomes practically the only form of political expression, or at least one that is always appropriate, making a real political assessment of any particular situation unnecessary. And since illegality requires a lot of commitment and courage, it in great part suffices to define the identity of the group. In brief, they over-simplify the problem. But no more so than those who in similar fashion mystify pacifism and voting. Victorious movements are ones that can adapt to circumstances, use violence when really necessary, but also humour, music, reason, and patience. Which can be stubborn in one case and negotiate in another. Flexibility is the secret of survival for any living thing."

But flexibility towards the outside is founded on flexibility within the movement. To pose the question of the community is to pose the question of flexible engagement among its different components, it is to pose the question of acknowledgement of the inevitable limits of one's preferred methods of struggles, and therefore acknowledgement of the 'other'. To pose the question of flexibility and community is to pose the question of an unprecedented maturity of a global movement.

COMMUNITY OF COMMUNITIES: LOCAL AND GLOBAL STRUGGLES

In dealing with the contingent question of 'violence' and of 'alternatives', our starting point is the same, the constitution of community: an inclusive horizontal relation to the other based on respect, autonomy, solidarity and responsibility. Here I don't want to refer to the 'real' communities we find ourselves in: professional communities, business communities, housing communities, work communities, local communities. Often, these refer to an idealised representation of a cluster of people who have something in common: a profession, a business, a house, a job, and a locality. In this definition of community, this something in common outweighs the rest. In a sense, all the rest is subordinated to this common character. For example, how many times have we heard the rhetoric of the 'company community': we (i.e. we workers and managers spread over a hierarchy of pay and command) are all in the same company, we are the community of people working in this company, we need to reach an understanding, we need to put aside our disagreements (over pay and work conditions, over authority, over privileges and rights) because we are a community, and we have to focus on the competitive struggle against others.

The community I am referring to is not dependent on a sociological condition that is common to a group of people. That kind of community can always be instrumentally manipulated. Any single characteristic defining my commonality with another, is based on silence concerning a million other differences with the same others. Why is it that in that context and that time, this single characteristics was selected to express commonality? What is the political meaning of this selection? How did power relations inform that selection? (And the other way around, any single characteristics defining my difference with another are based on the silence concerning a million other commonalties with the same other).

Instead, the community I am talking about is a form of engagement with the other. It transcends locality, job, social condition, gender, age, race, culture, sexual orientation, language, religion and beliefs. It makes all of this of secondary importance to the constitution of communal relations. Indeed, all these criteria present themselves only as raw materials, as presuppositions of a mode of engagement with the other.

Isn't this the blurred shape of the world of which we dream? How can we make it come true? If only more were to join us, if only other communities, at work, in localities, in neighbourhoods, could join in with their richness, their humour and their problems. If only we did not counterpoise our struggles to the daily struggle in which each man, woman and child on this earth engages on a daily basis.

The debate over tactics thus must make the great leap. It is not a question of choosing between the big demos on occasions of big summits that attract media attention and going back to campaign in our localities. No, this is again a false opposition. Our big demos would not be possible without the universe of our local struggles, and big demos are important for us because they produce networks, face to face contacts, friendships, and human bonding. Yet, our local struggles are nothing without the continuous and insistent connection with all the rest, and local struggles are important because it is there that our desires and aspirations take shape. The global scene for us is the discovery of the 'other', while the local scene is the discovery of the 'us'. But then, by discovering the 'other', we change the sense of the 'us', and by discovering the 'us', we change our relation to the 'other'. In a community, commonality is a creative process of discovery, not a presupposition. So, we do both, but we do it having the community in mind, the community as a mode of engagement with the other. When we organise the next big demo on the occasion of their summits, we need to keep this in mind. Before thinking about stewards to police the demos, let us spend more time with the local community ahead of time, 'us' meaning all people believing in different tactics, 'violent' and 'non-violent'. Let us go there, talk to them, ask them what is the level of confrontation they, who live there, would like to see on the ground. Would they be sorry to see their streets devastated, their cars destroyed, their phone boxes burned? You know, not everybody has an insurance policy, and to some people a car is a life tool, not just a status symbol. In some places, it may take months to replace a local post office, a phone box or even a branch of a bank? Can we engage in discussion on these terms, concretising the question of 'violence' and 'non-violence', bringing it to the ground, near the real needs and real lives of people? Can we talk about their problems and our problems, their aspirations and our aspirations? What are the grassroots unions saying, what are neighbourhood associations saying? Can we all ask ourselves and debate the purpose of the next demo and whether should we continue with ritualised practices (whether 'violent' or 'non-violent'), risking turning the entire movement into a yawning mass? Or maybe they think that a bit of mess on the street is exactly what they need. Who knows what will be the emerging answers? In a community practising democracy we can talk about everything, so long as in practice we respect each other.

Ultimately, the point is that the only right tactic is one that emerges out of a communal process of engagement with the other. Incidentally, the only 'right' world is also the one that emerges out of this process of recognition of the other. And in this world, the distinction of local and global is not a distinction between 'community' and the outside, but between 'communities' and 'community of communities'.

This article has been taken from www.thecommoner.org

staying on the streets

by S T A R H A W K

Since Genoa, there has been lots of healthy debate about where the move-ment needs to go. The large scale protests are becoming more dangerous and difficult. The summits are moving to inaccessible locations. The IMF and the World Bank and the G8 and the WTO continue to do their business. Are we being effective enough to justify the risks we're taking? Should we be focusing more on local work, building our day-to-day networking and organising? I was in Genoa. Because of what I experienced there, including the moments of real terror and horror, I am more convinced than ever that we need to stay in the streets. We need to continue mounting large actions, contesting summits, working on the global scale.

Our large scale actions have been extraordinarily effective. I've heard despair-ing counsels that the protests have not affected the debates in the G8 or the WTO or the IM/World Bank. In fact they have, they have significantly changed the agendas and the propaganda issuing forth. In any case, the actual policies of these institutions will be the last thing to change. But for most of us on the streets, changing the debate within these institutions is not our purpose. Our purpose is to undercut their legit-imacy, to point a spotlight at their programs and policies, and to raise the social costs of their existence until they become insupportable. Contesting the summits has delegitimised these institutions in a way no local organising possibly can. The big summit meetings are elaborate rituals, ostentatious shows of power that reinforce the entitlement and authority of the bodies they represent. When those bodies are forced to meet behind walls, to fight a pitched battle over every conference, to retreat to isolated locations, the ritual is interrupted and their legitimacy is undercut. The agree-ments that were being negotiated in secret are brought out into the spotlight of public

scrutiny. The lie that globalisation means democracy is exposed; and the mask of benevolence is ripped off. Local organising simply can't do this as effectively as the big demonstrations. Local organising is vital, and there are other things it does do: outreach, education, movement building, the creation of viable alternatives, the amelioration of some of the immediate effects of global policy. We can't and won't abandon the local, and in fact never have: many of us work on both scales. No-one can go to every summit: we all need to root ourselves in work in our own communities. But many of us have come to the larger, global actions because we understand that the trade agreements and institutions we contest are designed to undo all of our local work and override the decisions and aspirations of local communities. We can make it a conscious goal of every large scale action to strengthen local networks and support local organising. Aside from Washington DC, Brussels, or Geneva, which have no choice, no city is ever going to host one of these international meetings twice. Even now, we hear rumours that Washington is considering relocating or limiting the upcoming IMF/World Bank meeting. But if we find ways to organise mass actions that leave resources and functioning coalitions behind, then each grand action can strengthen and support the local work that continues on a daily basis.

Summits won't remain the nice, juicy, targets that they are for long. Over the last two years, we've reaped an agenda of meetings that were set and contracted for before Seattle. Now that they are locating the meetings in ever more obscure and isolated venues, we need a strategy that can allow us to continue building momentum. As an example, some of us have been talking about linked, large-scale regional actions targeting stock exchanges and financial institutions when the WTO meets in Qatar in November. The message we'll be sending is: "If you move the summits beyond our reach, and continue the policies of power consolidation and wealth concentration, then social unrest will spread beyond these specific institutions to challenge the whole structure of global corporate capitalism itself." Marches, teach-ins, countersummits, programs of positive alternatives alone can't pose this level of threat to the power structure, but combined with direct action on the scale we've now reached, they can. Of course, the more successful we are, the meaner they get. But when they use force against us, we still win, even though the victory comes at a high cost. Systems of power maintain themselves through our fear of the force they can command, but force is costly. They cannot sustain themselves if they have to actually use force in order to accomplish every normal function.

Genoa was a victory won at a terrible price. I hope never to undergo another night like I spent when they raided the IMC and the Diaz school, knowing that atrocities were being done just across the way and not being able to stop them. I ache and grieve and rage over the price. I would do almost anything to assure that no-one, especially no young person, ever suffers such brutality again. Almost anything. Anything except backing away from the struggle. Because that level of violence and brutality is being enacted, daily, all over the world. It's the shooting of four students in New Guinea, the closing of a school in Senegal, the work quota in a *maquiladora* on the Mexican border, the clearcutting of a forest in Oregon, the price of privatised water in Cochabamba. It's the violence being perpetrated on the bodies of youth, especially youth of colour, in prisons all over the United States, and the brutality and murder going on in Colombia, Palestine, Venezuela and it's the utter disregard for the integrity of the ecosystems that sustain us all.

I don't see the choice as being between the danger of a large action and safety. I no longer see any place of safety. Or rather, I see that in the long run our safest course is to act strongly now. The choice is about when and how we contest the powers that are attempting to close all political space for true dissent. Genoa made clear that they will fight ruthlessly to defend the consolidation of their power, but we still have a broad space in which to organise and mount large actions. We need to defend that space by using it, filling and broadening it. Either we continue to fight them together now when we can mount large-scale, effective actions, or we fight them later in small, isolated groups, or alone when they break down the doors of our homes in the middle of the night. Either we wage this struggle when there are still living forests, running rivers, and resilience left in the life support systems of the planet, or we fight when the damage is even deeper and the hope of healing slim.

We have many choices about how to wage the struggle. We can be more strategic, more creative, more skilful in what we do. We can learn to better prepare people for what they might face, and to better support people afterwards. We have deep questions to consider about violence and non-violence, about our tactics and our long range vision.

But those choices remain only so long as we keep open the space in which to make them. We need to grow, not shrink. We need to explore and claim new political territory. We need the actions of this autumn to be bigger, wilder, more creatively outrageous and inspiring than ever, from the IMF/World Bank actions in Washington DC at the end of September to the many local and regional actions in November when the WTO meets in Quatar. We need to stay in the streets.

ASKING THE RIGHT QUESTIONS

Genoa was a watershed for the anti-globalisation movement. It's clear now that this is a life or death struggle in the first world as it has always been in the third world. How we respond will determine whether repression destroys us or strengthens us. To come back stronger, we have to understand what actually happened there. The media are telling one story about Genoa: a small group of violent protestors got out of hand and the police overreacted. I've heard variations on this from within the movement: the Black Block was allowed to get out of hand to justify police violence. But that's not what happened in Genoa, and framing the problem that way will keep us focused on the wrong questions.

Let's be clear: in Genoa we encountered a carefully orchestrated political campaign of state terrorism. The campaign included disinformation, the use of infiltrators and provocateurs, collusion with avowed Fascist groups (and I don't mean fascist in the loose way the left sometimes uses the term, I mean Fascist as in 'direct inheritors of the traditions of Mussolini and Hitler'), the deliberate targeting of nonviolent groups for tear gas and beating, endemic police brutality, the torture of prisoners, the political persecution of the organisers, and a terrorist night raid on sleeping people by special forces wearing "Polizia" T-shirts under black sweatshirts, who broke bones, smashed teeth, and bashed in the skulls of non-resisting protestors.

They did all this openly, in a way that indicates they had no fear of repercussions and expected political protection from the highest sources. That expectation implicates not only the proto-Fascist Berlusconi regime of Italy, but by association the rest of the G8, especially the U.S. since it now appears that L.A. County Sheriffs helped train the most brutal of the special forces.

Italy has a history of the employment of such tactics, going back to the 'strategy of tension' used against the left in the 1970s, in fact, even further back to the 1920s and 1930s which don't seem all that far away any more once you've heard prisoners describe being tortured in rooms with pictures of Mussolini on the walls. Maybe even back to the Renaissance, if not the ancient Romans. The same tactics have, of course, been used extensively by U.S. agencies and other countries. Italy also has a political culture of highly confrontational actions and streetfighting with the police, as well as strong pacifist groups and groups like the Tute Bianche who are exploring new political territory that goes beyond the traditional definitions of violence and non-violence. All of this set the stage upon which the events of the G8 protest were played. The police used the Black Block, or more accurately, the myth and image of the Black Block, very effectively in Genoa, for their ends, not ours. Some aspects of Black Block tactics made that easy: the anonymity, the masks and easily identifiable dress code, the willingness to engage in more confrontational tactics and in property damage, and perhaps most significant, the lack of connection with the rest of the action and the organisers.

But the Black Block was not the source of the problem in Genoa. The problem was state, police and Fascist violence. Acts were done in Genoa, attributed to protes-

tors, that were irresponsible and wrong by anyone's standards—but it seems likely now that most of them were done by police. Or if not, police provocateurs were so endemic that it's impossible to tell what might have been done by people in our movement or to hold anyone accountable. So the issue Genoa presents us with is not 'How do we control the violent elements among us?', although that conceivably might be an issue someday. It's 'How do we forestall another campaign of lies, police-instigated violence, and retaliation?

There's no easy answer to that question. The simplest strategy would be to go back to a strict form of non-violence, which many people are proposing. I don't know why I find myself in resistance to that answer. I'm a longtime advocate of non-violence, I have no intention of ever throwing a brick through a window or lobbing a rock at a cop myself, and in general I think breaking windows and fighting cops in a mass action is counterproductive at best and suicidal at worst. One reason might be that I can no longer use the same word to describe what I've seen even the most unruly elements of our movement do in actions and what the cops did in Genoa. If breaking windows and fighting back when the cops attack is 'violence', then give me a new word, a word a thousand times stronger, to use when the cops are beating non-resisting people into comas.

Another might be just that I like the Black Block. I've been in many actions now where the Black Block was a strong presence. In Seattle I was royally pissed off at them for what I saw as their unilateral decision to violate agreements everyone else accepted. In Washington in 2000, I saw that they abided by guidelines they disagreed with and had no part in making, and I respected them for it. I've sat under the hooves of the police horses with some of them when we stopped a sweep of a crowded street using tactics Gandhi himself could not have criticised. I've choked with them in the tear gas in Quebec City and seen them refrain from property damage there when confronted by local people. I'm bonded. Yes, there have been times I've been furious with some of them, but they're my comrades and allies in this struggle and I don't want to see them excluded or demonised. We need them, or something like them. We need room in the movement for rage, for impatience, for militant fervour, for an attitude that says "We are badass, kickass folks and we will tear this system down." If we cut that off, we devitalise ourselves.

We also need the Gandhian pacifists. We need room for compassion, for faith, for an attitude that says, "My hands will do the works of mercy and not the works of war." We need those who refuse to engage in violence because they do not want to live in a violent world. And we need space for those of us who are trying to explore forms of struggle that fall outside the categories. We need radical creativity, space to experiment, to carve out new territory, invent new tactics, make mistakes.

There are campaigns being waged now that are defined as clearly and strictly non-violent: the School of the Americas, Vandenberg, Vieques, among others. Those guidelines have been respected, and no black-clad brick-throwing figures have attempted to impose other tactics. But the actions directed against the big summits have drawn their strength from a much broader political spectrum, from unions and NGOs to anarchist revolutionaries. All these groups feel a certain ownership of the issue and the fat, juicy targets that the summits represent.

How do we create a political space that can hold these contradictions, and still survive the intense repression directed against us? How do we go where no social movement has ever gone before?

Maybe these are the questions we really need to ask. In a life or death situation, there's a great temptation to attempt to exert more control, to set rules, to police each other, to retreat to what seems like safe ground. But all my instincts tell me that going back to what seems safe and tried and true is a mistake. As an anarchist, I'm not interested in doing any kind of police work. I want to call each other to greater, not lesser freedom, knowing that also means greater responsibility and greater risk.

Using provocateurs to instigate violence which can be blamed on dissenters and used to justify repression is a time-tested, generally successful way of destroying radical movements. But it's a strategy that thrives on the familiar, the expected. Identifying provocateurs in the midst of an action is like trying to spray for a pest in the garden: the toxicity of the spray, of the suspicion, secrecy and lack of trust, may be as great as that of the pest.

But plants can resist pests if they are grown in healthy soil. To forestall infiltration and provocateurs, we need to examine the soil of our movement. I'd like to suggest three nutrients that can make us more pest resistant: communication, solidarity and creativity. We have to be in communication. We can no longer afford to wage parallel but disconnected struggles at the same demonstration. We need to clearly state our intentions and goals for each action, and ask others to support them. We may need to argue and struggle with each, to negotiate, to compromise. Articulating a clear set of agreements about tactics may at times be the best way to forestall provocateurs. But agreements are only agreements when everyone participates in making them. If one wing of the movement attempts to impose them, they are not agreements but decrees, and moreover, decrees that will not be respected and that we have no power to enforce.

That communication involves risk on both sides, but those risks have to be taken, intelligently and thoughtfully, of course. We need to put a higher priority on our communication than on our standing with our funding sources or our security culture. If my tactic of choice makes it impossible for me to talk to you, I need to question whether it's an appropriate tactic for a mass action.

In that dialogue, we actually have to struggle to respect each other. No-one gets to claim the moral high ground. None of us get to exclusively set the agenda, determine the form of what we do or decree the politics. Those who advocate non-violence, a chief tenet of which is to respect your opponent, need to practise it within the movement. You can't just dismiss the Black Block and other militant groups as 'negative rebels' or immature adolescents acting out. They have a political perspective that is serious, thoughtful, and deserves to be taken seriously.

But it also means that more militant groups need to stop dismissing those who advocate non-violence as middle-class, passive, and cowardly. The Black Block is widely respected for its courage, but it takes another kind of courage to sit down in front of the riot cops without sticks or rocks or Molotovs. It takes courage to have your identity known, to organise in your own city where you can't disappear but must stand and face the consequences. 'Non-violent' does not equate with 'non-confrontational', or with wanting to be safe on the sidelines. The essence of non-violent political struggle is to create intense confrontations that highlight the violence in the system, and then to stand and openly take the consequences. In today's repressive climate, where 88 year old nuns are being given year-long prison sentences for completely pacific actions, the risks of non-violence may be much higher than the risks of anonymous street fighting.

We need to communicate clearly with the larger community as well, proactively, not reactively. We have to let people know what our intentions are and what the parameters of the action might be. Imagine the Black Block putting out a Crimestopper leaflet: "If you see a group of masked figures looting small shops, burning private cars, and endangering your children... get their badge numbers! They are the cops! Because we're the Black Block, and that's not what we do." We need to talk to the not-already-converted, door to door, face to face, not to lecture them but to ask about their lives and the effects these issues have on them, and to ask them to show support for us.

We need to be in real solidarity with each other. Solidarity is not just about refraining from denouncing each other to the media, or holding vigils for those in jail. It means putting the good of the whole above our immediate individual desires or even safety. It means supporting each other's intentions and goals, even when we only partially agree with them. Not just by saying, "you do your thing and I'll do mine," but by actually taking responsibility for our actions and for the impact they have on others beyond ourselves or our immediate group. Greater freedom demands greater responsibility. In a mass action individual decisions have a collective impact.

Some tactics are like the loud-voiced guy in the meeting: they take up all the available space and make it impossible for anyone else to be heard. Cops are not creatures of fine distinctions. If one group is throwing Molotov cocktails and smashing shop windows, it may well affect how the police react to the pacifist group a block over. The community, too, may miss the subtle difference between burning the neighbourhood bank and burning the neighbourhood store. So, just as the loud guy has to learn to step back occasionally and shut up to give others a chance to be heard, high confrontation tactics sometimes need to be restrained just to allow other possibilities to exist.

Solidarity is about what we do on the street. It means protecting each other as best we can, and certainly not deliberately endangering each other. Of course, one group's idea of protection may be another group's idea of endangerment. A barricade may seem protective, but if your strategy is to deescalate tension, a barricade may actually make your situation more dangerous. We need to respect each other's choices. Solidarity means that if I'm sitting down in front of a line of riot cops and you're behind me, I can trust that you're restraining the crowd behind from trampling me, not throwing a rock over my head. And that if you push through a line of cops and I'm behind you, I'm there to support you, not restrain you. We have a right to ask for solidarity from everyone who wants to be out on the street together.

Solidarity is also about holding each other accountable, critiquing what we do together with the purpose of learning from our mistakes and becoming more effective. Critiquing is not attacking: a good critique is a mark of respect, it's saying, "I know that you and I share a common interest in making this work better." Perhaps most of all, we need to be creative. Maybe, just to stimulate our thinking, we need to mount one action with one simple guideline: No tired, overused tactics allowed. No cross-the-line symbolic arrests, no bricks through the windows of Starbucks. And please, please, no boring chants that have been recycled since the Vietnam War, if not before. ("Hey hey, ho ho, King George the Third has got to go?") At least this would be a useful thought experiment. We need to think outside the fences and the boxes. We need to do the unexpected, change clothes, change tactics, be where they don't expect us to be, doing what they don't expect us to do. If they expect us to trash McDonalds, we're there disrupting its operations by giving out free food and asking the workers how globalisation affects them. If they expect militants to dress in black, then the militants go lavender and the pacifists stage a Funeral for Democracy, surrounding the White House dressed in black mourning and veils. If they expect us to walk up quietly in groups of five to get arrested, we disappear and reappear somewhere else entirely. If the hardcore streetfighters pull down a fence, the 88 year old nuns are the first through into the Red Zone. If they block off the meeting and concentrate their defences on a wall, we claim the rest of the city. If they hide the summits in inaccessible locations, we choose our own turf.

These are hard challenges, but these are hard times, too and they're not getting easier. I've already seen too many movements splinter and fail or grandstand themselves to death in ever more extreme and suicidal acts, or suffocate from self-righteous moralism. I want to win this revolution. I don't think we have the ecological and social leeway to mount another one if this fails. And the odds of winning are so slim that we can't afford to be anything but smart, strategic, and tight with one another. We need to stand shoulder to shoulder, even when we disagree. And if we can do that, if we can hold these differences within our movement, we'll have taken a step toward meeting the much greater challenges we'll face when we do win, and come to remake a deeply diverse world.

www.starhawk.org (thanks to Lisa Fithian, Hilary McQuie ad David Miller for discussions that contributed to this piece.)

beyond genoa –where to now?

by RICHARD K MOORE

WILL A DEATH IN THE FAMILY BREATHE LIFE INTO THE MOVEMENT?

Seattle may have been some sort of watershed, but Carlo's killing in Genoa is a turning point for the anti-capitalist movement (if we can call it that). How we play it from here will have repercussions far beyond the blood-stained streets of Northern Italy. It was no freak cub-cop overreaction that left one mother mourning and several others preparing to, as the sun hit the sea on Friday night, but a deliberate act of terror—in the most basic sense of the word.

The snowball that's been gaining weight and speed as it rolled through Geneva, Prague and Gothenburg has become far too jagged a spike in the side of those steering the planetary carve-up. So bullets meet brains—and young people are shot dead for daring to think there can be another way.

The message from the world's authorities is clear: go back to your homes, do not meddle in what doesn't concern you, return to your televisions, to smoking dope and stealing traffic cones and leave the intricacies of global economics alone—because if you don't we will kill you. The same way we killed Carlo Giuliani.

For decades, the poorest of the planet's families from Asia, Africa and Latin America have been burying the fathers, the sisters and the first-born sons who have dared to confront the forces of global capitalism. But Carlo's death spells something different. For the first time the global elite has begun to kill the children of its own

people. Dissent will no longer be tolerated. The whip of economic dictatorship is finally cracking at home.

But where we go from here is still up for grabs. The globalisers would dearly love to see us run scared, or split our ranks with paranoid accusations of 'whose side are you on?' Tactical difference should not be confused with police-collusion and counter-revolutionary activity... or vice-versa.

True enough, there were cops in ski-masks leading the more excitable and naive among Genoa's young bloods on attacks on corner shops, bus stops and post offices. But the agitators can be addressed. If everyone who takes any action knows why they are taking it and what sort of action they think is necessary to achieve their goal, then the police will not be able to steer the crowds, the meetings, the discussion groups or 'the movement' as a whole. The problem is less one of infiltration, more one of focus.

The more liberal elements of groups such as the Genoa Social Forum (GSF) or Prague's INPEG, need to understand that just because they have the ear of the newspapers, it doesn't mean they speak with the voice of the people. The reformist agenda of these groups, who call for more legislation, more institutions and stronger government control over the runaway capitalist train, is an entire philosophy away from the genuine participatory democracy sought by many.

Instead of calling for the deployment of "non-violent methods of restraining and defusing violent behaviour" for those who fail to adhere to "the political and ethical parameters of our mass actions" (Walden Bello, I expected so much more from you), perhaps the up-in-arms brigade should be questioning their own attempted coup of the global resistance movement. Both INPEG and the GSF produced documents laying down 'rules' for 'participation' in what were illegal blockades of international meetings. The GSF tactical manifesto was insulting to the resistance history of many of its signatory groups. The anarchists were perhaps the only people (police included) who took to the streets with honest intentions, both about their goals and what they were prepared to do to achieve them. The anarchists have long been aware that power (be it economic or governmental) is the problem—not who holds it— and needs, therefore, to be removed altogether. The Black Block do not "detract from 'the message'"—they have a different message. And unlike the liberals and the hierarchical groups of the organised left who would, at best, replace those in power with their own institutions manned by their own people, and at worst, settle for a seat at the G8 table, the anarchists' message is not a lunge for the throne shrouded in the smoke screen language of 'justice' and 'liberty'. The anarchists recognise that a power-wielding state is no better than a power-wielding corporation, and they are well aware that the police are the front-line defence for both.

This is not to dispel organisation. Organisation is imperative. Co-operation and communication between the disparate groups involved in the resistance is key. But an insurrectionary pseudo-government (complete with pseudo-police if Walden gets his way)? Hmmm... two legs good, four legs bad time already.

The strength of this movement/loose-amalgamation-of-people-who-ain't-taking-any-more-shit, has always been its leaderless fluidity, its constantly changing strategy, its unpredictable tactics and targets. This is why the authorities (until now) have found it so hard to get a handle on what we were up to—we weren't following patterns or playing by any discernible rules. Now, as we witnessed in Genoa, the Man has caught up. Infiltration is the price of protesting-by-numbers. Though Italy was an ideal venue for us to mobilise an unprecedented number of insurrectionaries, it was also a touch for the global authorities who could mobilise one of the West's most corrupt, right wing and violent state security forces. Recent history has shown the Italian security services are prepared to stoop to anything in order to undermine subversive movements. Genoa proved they haven't lost their touch.

The point has been made that if the non-violent protesters came up with something that worked maybe more people would adopt their tactics. However, non-violence should not be confused with not rocking the boat—as often appears to be the case. Those who feel the 'violent anarchists' are curbing their successes should maybe look at how successful their own tactics are. It is no coincidence that Tony Blair "welcomes" peaceful calls for debt reform—the communiqués are duly issued, the lip service paid, and then... nothing changes, and the global carve-up getting mapped in the Oval office doesn't miss a step.

Maybe time within the 'movement' would be better spent skipping the anarchist witch-hunt and focusing on our common enemies. One of the more eye opening moments in Genoa came when the non-violent protesters and the Black Block crossed paths. At around three o'clock on July 20th, an anarchist block had tried to cross the Piazza Manin en route to the Red Zone, the non-violent white handed pacifists in the square refused to let them pass. Discussions between the two groups were interrupted by a vicious police attack during which the white hand protesters sat down hands aloft and took a severe beating without fighting back (as is their prerogative). However an hour later when three masked youths walked back through the square the (understandably upset) pacifists threw first a stick, then a bottle, then a rock at them. They saw the Black Block as the cause for their pain. No violence had been directed at the police wielding the boots, the clubs and the teargas, but strict pacifist adherence could be suspended in order to attack anyone (without authority) who had not stuck to their tactical code. Perhaps this pacifist submission to authority says more about the authoritarian nature of the society they seek, than about their abhorrence of the Black Block's tactics.

The more reasoned voices of Italy's Ya Basta collective are already admitting the error of attacking the brick-throwers (there is something twisted about an elite Tute Bianche hit squad in Subcommandante Marcos T-shirts beating people with crash helmets for wearing bandannas over their faces). However, the security services will no doubt be fuelling the fire of division and will embrace the peace-policers (as they did in the US during the anti Vietnam protests of the 1960s) who, they hope in turn, will return the anti-capitalist front-line to the letters pages of the *Washington Post*.

The rats inside the global Red Zone want us to crawl back to our workplaces, to the fear of unemployment and to the gratitude for an irregular playtime. But we can say no. We can say: we do not care how well protected you are with your armies, your police, your banks or your brands, because we have had enough and we will not run from your guns.

These would-be leaders can scuttle off to Qatar or cruise ships or Rocky Mountain retreats, but we know their meetings have little impact on the real decisions made elsewhere. Perhaps we in the West should follow the example of India's farmers who removed Monsanto's headquarters brick by brick and took it away. If we don't like Bush's missile defence plans, we could go to Fylingdales and take it away brick by brick, bullet by bullet. We have the ability to take capitalism out piece by piece, pound by pound. We could pick a company, say Balfour Beatty, and put them out of business. A thousand actions at a thousand sites dismantling every facet of their insidious business. Would their shareholders bail them out? Unlikely. Then we could move on and up. When we can co-ordinate our actions as millions of people, then maybe we can dismantle the oil industry, the arms industry, the jail industry, the government industry?

The mass street actions we have been able to mount and the dedication, planning and application of those on the streets has shown us that we have the wherewithal to make decisions and carry them out regardless of what the state may think or threaten. If we put this dynamic to work away from the mega-summits we can become a threat again. But we need to be imaginative and we need to stay ahead of the beast. Where we choose to go from here is crucial to whether we are in the process of sparking serious global change or whether we are merely in the death throes of another cycle of resistance.

If we don't want corporate activity in our neighbourhoods, let's chuck the corporations out. If we don't want the police or the government flexing their muscle in our neighbourhoods, let's stop recognising their bogus authority and encourage others to do the same. Let's link our communities together—not through state or

WE DON'T ONLY CRY FOR THE DEAD
TURN SADNESS AND ANGER
INTO RESISTANCE!

business initiatives—but through people who share a common struggle. If we believe in making changes and creating something better, and if we are prepared to take the risks and put in the time, then let's do it. Let's not allow Carlo's death to be in vain. Because when one of us catches a bullet, a club or jail sentence, a little bit of all of us dies. But together we are alive and together we can, and we will, win.

You make plans, we make HISTORY

contacts

*"Meaningful action, for revolutionaries, is whatever increases the
confidence, the autonomy, the initiative, the participation, the
solidarity, the equalitarian tendencies and the self-activity of the
working class, and whatever assists in their demystification.
Sterile and harmful activity is whatever reinforces the passivity of the
working classes, their apathy, their cynicism, their differentiation
through hierarchy, their alienation, their reliance on others to do things
for them and the degree to which they can therefore be manipulated—
even by those allegedly acting on their behalf"*

If you want to find out what is going on, we recommend that you contact indymedia (www.indymedia.org.uk). Two other excellent sources of information are
SchNews (c/o On the Fiddle, PO Box 2600, Brighton BN2 2DX; e-mail: schnews
@brighton.co.uk; http://www.schnews.org.uk) and Counter-Information (c/o Trans-
mission, 28 King Street, Glasgow, G1 5QP, Scotland; counterinfo @punk.org.uk).

If you want to get hold of books and magazines (and about everything else
apart from the kitchen sink), we recommend that you contact the following: AK Distribution, PO Box 12766, Edinburgh, EH8 9YE (www.akuk.com) and Active Distribution, BM Active, London, WC1N 3XX (www.activedistribution.org).

There are many groups around the country who share to greater or lesser
degrees the politics expressed in *On Fire*. Among the more 'national' based groups
are the Anarchist Federation (c/o 84b Whitechapel High Street, London E1 7QX;
acf@burn.ucsd.edu), Class War (PO Box 467, London E8 3QX) and the Solidarity
Federation (PO Box 29, SW PDO, Manchester M15 5HW).

One group worth getting into touch with for their sense of style and imagination is the Wombles, trying to develop new tactics for taking our struggles forward.
Check their website www.wombleaction.mrnice.net

Two of the best from a more ecological/anarchist perspective are Earth First!
(Earth First! Action Update is available from c/o Cornerstone Resource Centre,

16 Sholebroke Avenue, Leeds LS7 3HB; http://www.k2net.co.uk.ef/) and Reclaim the Streets (PO Box 9656, London N4 4JY; e-mail: rts@gn.apc.org.).

There are many local groupings—for a comprehensive list of local groups, get *The Agitator* from PO Box 2474, London, N8 (cost £1.50 including postage), or go online to: http:/hsg.cupboard.org. Some of the local groups include 56 Info shop, 56 Crampton Street, London, SE17, Anarchist Teapot, PO Box 4144, Worthing, West Sussex, BN14 7NZ, Autonomous Centre of Edinburgh, 17 West Montgomery Place, Edinburgh, EH7 5HA, Bradford 1 in 12 Club, 21/23 Albion Street, Bradford, West Yorkshire, BD1, Haringay Solidarity Group, PO Box 2474, London, N8, Kebele Kulture Projekt, 14 Robertson Road, Eastville, Bristol, BS5 6YT, Leicester Radical Alliance, Dept Z, Littlethorn Bookshop, Humberside Gate, Leicester, LE1 1WB, People Not Profit, c/o News from Nowhere, 96 Bold Street, Liverpool, L1 and West London Anarchists and Radicals, c/o BM Makhno, London, WC1N 3XX.

Alternatively if you have Internet access, an excellent starting place is the AUT-OP-SY discussion list and website:

http://lists.village.virginia.edu/~spoons/aut_html/.

Other sites of interest include

http://www.spunk.org/

http://www.hrc.wmin.ac.uk/guest/radical/LINKS.HTM

http://flag.blackened.net/revolt/revolt.html

http://www.midnightnotes.org/

http://www.geocities.com/CapitolHill//Lobby/3909/index.html

http://www.geocities.com/CapitolHill/Lobby/2379/

http://www.geocities.com/Athens/Acropolis/8195/

None of these groups or publications are perfect, but if you can cut through the bullshit and jargon, they can all be useful in one way or another.

One Off Press
September 2001

We would like to thank everyone who assisted in putting this book together: writing articles, commenting on what had been written, providing photographs, doing the design, raising the money needed to cover the cost of printing. Everyone has put in work for free and no-one is receiving any money from selling this book. On Fire is being sold as cheaply as possible to make it as accessible as possible. If any money is made, then it will be either used to pay for another print run or given to appropriate anti-capitalist struggles. We would particularly like to thank Active Distribution, AK Distribution and Flat Earth Records for their financial assistance

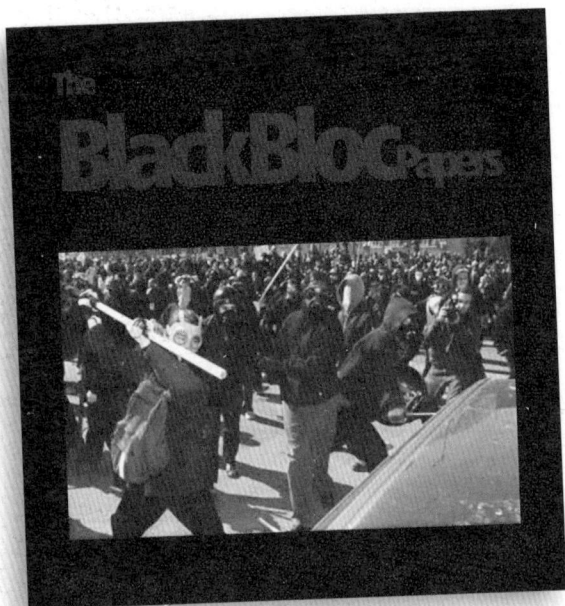

The Black Bloc Papers

An Anthology of Primary Texts from the North American Anarchist Black Bloc

Uncompromising polemics & gripping images from the frontlines of the battle against global capitalism.

The Black Bloc are the most militant — and misrepresented — segment of the growing anti-capitalist movement. Here are the collected communiqués issued by the Bloc after every major street action of the past year. They've circulated widely in the underground and are now available all together for the first time to a wider audience, with commentary from the Green Mountain Anarchist Collective.

A passionate manifesto in the rhetorical tradition of the Situationists, the book includes an analysis of the meaning of Black Bloc street actions in the context of the larger global anti-capitalist movement, and a call for greater tactical development among protestors.

With twenty pages of photos from the actions discussed, The Black Bloc Papers is a crucial document in the history they're about to write us out of, and an indispensable guide to the militant road ahead. Collectors' item or pocket bomb? It's up to you.

Available from AK Press in Spring 2002

AK Press (U.K.)
P.O. Box 12766
Edinburgh EH8 9YE Scotland
www.akuk.com

AK Press (U.S.)
674-A 23rd Street
Oakland, CA 94612
www.akpress.org

Check out our website(s) or write for a mail-order catalogue.

see em, screen em, bury em in ya boss's skull

GUERILLAVISION PRESENTS

guerillavision@angelfire.com

also available from schnews@brighton.co.uk

STILL AVAILABLE TO BUY & BOOTLEG ON VHS VIDEO

BIG RATTLE IN SEATTLE • N30

23 minutes of incitement and inspiration from the N30 uprising against the WTO. An angry tide of dissent finally draws a line in the sand. Enough. A must see for all budding revolutionaries

CAPITALS ILL • DK IN DC • A16

As capitalism s demise draws closer, 20,000 take to the streets of Washington DC to stop the World Bank & IMF in their murdering motherfucking tracks. 20 minutes. The scaffold is built, the basket is ready

CROWD BITES WOLF • S26

The Czech Connection: The Bank & Fund scuttle off to Prague, but an international army of insurrection is waiting. Caught in the middle, one man finds his anticipated fortnight on the piss shelved by a chance encounter...23 minutes

EAch TaPE is £5 PLus £1 in STAmpS (FOR POSTAGE). BUY ALL 3 AND GET POSTAGE FOR £2. FROM: GuERiLLaVisioN, Box 91, GreEn LeAf bOOkshop, 82 ColsTON sT, brisTOL, bS1 5BB

or further info email:
uerillavision@angelfire.com
where possible email to
onfirm order postage
ach tape comes with a
ull colour cover

Concealed cash only. No cheques
All tapes are PAL VHS, but email if you want NTSC/mini DV

you're
in there
for us
we're
out here
for you

SUPPORT ALL
ANTI-CAPITALIST &
CLASS STRUGGLE
PRISONERS

GET THE UPDATED LIST OF PRISONERS FROM SCHNEWS
PO BOX 2600, BRIGHTON, BN2 2DX. www.schnews.org.uk